DATA BANK ON INDIAN ECONOMY

DATA BANK
ON
INDIAN ECONOMY

Compiled and Edited by

Arvind M. Dwivedi

ANMOL PUBLICATIONS PVT. LTD.

NEW DELHI - 110 002 (INDIA)

ANMOL PUBLICATIONS PVT. LTD.
4374/4B, Ansari Road, Daryaganj
New Delhi-110 002
www.anmolbooks.com

Data Bank on Indian Economy

First Edition 2001
ISBN 81-261-1001-5

PRINTED IN INDIA

Published by J. L. Kumar for Anmol Publications Pvt. Ltd., New Delhi-110 002 and Printed at Tarun Offset Press, Delhi.

CONTENTS

PREFACE

Today, we are living in the age of competitions. Gone are the days when the degrees were enough to get a job. Now the thorough study of any subject is required to get through in any competitive examination. The objective multiple choice type questions are asked almost in all the competitions. In nutshell, this technique is popular to assess the candidates' knowledge of a particular subject. In order to meet the increasing demand of the aspirants, we have prepared the Data Bank on Indian Economy and feel pleasure on presenting the same before you. It is concise, comprehensive and dependable which has a wide coverage of the syllabus.

The proportion, of questions from Economics in General study has get tremendous increase in the recent past. Near about 15% questions are asked from this portion. In the present data bank we have touched all the corners of syllabus as well as the latest pattern of questions asked in UPSC, SSC, LIC, GIC, CDS, NDA and other examinations. We have taken utmost care in preparing the questions with particular gradation and level of the various examination.

To enhance the utility of the book and to make it more informative, the readers can send their comments and suggestions which will be incorporated in the subsequent editions of the book.

—Arvind M. Dwivedi

1
INDIAN ECONOMY: AN INTRODUCTION

1. Meaning of the word economic is most closely connected with the word
   (a) Unlimited (b) Extravagant
   (c) Scarce (d) Restricted.

2. A theory of
   (a) An assumption
   (b) A validated hypothesis
   (c) A "if-then" proposition
   (d) A hypothesis .

3. A hypothesis is tested by
   (a) Its ability to predict accurately
   (b) The realism of its assumption
   (c) The lack of realism of its assumption
   (d) None of the above.

4. "Economics is what economics do" was stated by
   (a) Alfred Marshall (b) Jacob Viner
   (c) R.W. Souter (d) Adam Smith.

5. Micro-economic theory studies how an economy determines
   (a) The price of economic resource
   (b) The price of services

(c) The price of goods
(d) All the above .

6. In which of the following periods the subject "Economics" was given the status of political economy" and was taught as a subject of social studies?
(a) Neo-classical period
(b) Mercantilist period
(c) Physiocratic period
(d) Classical period.

7. Which one of the follwoing economists called Economics as "gospel of Mammon"?
(a) Ruskin (b) Scilberton
(c) Thomas Carlyle (d) Scitovsky.

8. Micro-economic theory studies how a free-enterprise economy determines:
(a) The price of goods
(b) The price of economic resource
(c) The price of services
(d) All of the above.

9. The chief weakness in the Robinson Crusoe modes is that
(a) He did not exchange goods
(b) He did not use machinery
(c) He did not use money
(d) He had no capital.

10. The basic characteristic of a capitalistic economy is
(a) Full employment
(b) The private ownership of means of production
(c) An absence of monopoly
(d) Large-scale production in primary industries.

11. "Economics" the title was itself condemned as "a dismal science" as a "bastard science" and a "science of bread and butter" by
(a) Ruskin (b) R.A Meyer
(c) T.W Hutchinson (d) Kuznets.

12. Assume that the leading firms in an industry combine to carry out a common policy in their interest but that they keep their own separate identities such a combination is usually known as a
    (a) Cartel (b) Pure monopoly
    (c) Trust (d) Joint-stock company.

13. The situation in between the extremes of the government controlled planned economy and the perfectly free. Unplanned economy is known as a
    (a) Developed economy
    (b) Mixed economy
    (c) Capitaliset economy
    (d) Laissez Faire economy.

14. Ceteris peribus term is related to
    (a) Law of demand
    (b) Particle equilibrium theory
    (c) Monetary theory
    (d) All of the above.

15. A manufacturing firm would be classed as a pure monopoly if it were able to
    (a) Control the retail autlets for its product
    (b) Sell at a very low price
    (c) Exclude all potential competitors
    (d) Sell without advertising the product.

16. Assume that a farmer sells his produce to an agriculture marketing board. He is not allowed to sell to any other institution or to any other persons. In effect, the boards is from his view a
    (a) Oligopoly (b) Duopoly
    (c) Monopoly (d) Monopsony.

17. We may define economics as a study of problems arising from
    (a) The distribution of very scarce goods
    (b) Production , distribution and exchange

(c) Production and pricing of durable commodities
(d) Exchange of services for money.

18. The economist assumes that if a person must make the choice between one thing and another he will always choose the alternative that well
(a) Make him a more efficient worker
(b) Improve his future prospets
(c) Yields him the greater satisfaction
(d) Satisfy his wants without delay.

19. The consumer like the government must time after time allocate limited resources among large number of competing wants so as to achieve
(a) Optimum oppurtunity cost
(b) Average oppurtunity cost
(c) Freedom of exchange
(d) Maximum satisfaction.

20. An example of a market which approaches fairly near to perfection is
(a) The retail market
(b) The house market
(c) The labour market
(d) The foreign exchange market.

21. The fundamental economic problem being faced is one of
(a) Difference in the living standard of the people
(b) Decision making by the government
(c) Multiplicity of wants and scarcity of resources
(d) Shortage of labour.

22. Which aspect of taxation involves normative economics?
(a) The incidence of (i.e who actually pays for) the tax
(b) The effect of the tax on incentives to work
(c) The "fairness" of the tax
(d) All of the above.

23. In a free capitalistic society the allocation of the factors of production among the various productive activities is determined by
    (a) The pattern of consumer spending
    (b) The traditional employment of factors
    (c) Dicisions of the government
    (d) The wealth of entrepreneurs.

24. A person is obliged to choose between buying a sewing-machine and a radio. He buy the radio the oppurtunity cost of the radio may be said to be
    (a) The satisfaction obtained from its purchase
    (b) The sewing-machine he had to do without
    (c) The scarcity velue of the radio is money terms
    (d) The average cost of both the commodites.

25. In infrastructure of an economy we include
    (a) Power (b) Transport
    (c) Banking (d) All of the above.

26. In India all infrastructure
    (a) Is state monopoly
    (b) Is partially state monopoly
    (c) Is private owned
    (d) None of the above.

27. The market equilibrium for a commodity is determined by
    (a) The market demand for the commodity
    (b) The market supply of the commodity
    (c) The balancing of the forces of demand and supply for the commodity
    (d) All of the above.

28. In a free-enterprises economy the problems of what, how and for whom are solved by
    (a) A planning commitee
    (b) The elected representatives of the people
    (c) The price-mechanism
    (d) None of the above.

29. The important characteristics of a mixed economic system are

    (a) Co-existence of public and private sector
    (b) Use of market-mechanism in the private sector
    (c) Use of economic planning
    (d) Government regulation and control of the economy
    (e) All of the above.

30. The fundamental economic problem being faced is one of

    (a) Diufference in the living standard of the people
    (b) Decision-making by the standard of the people
    (c) Multiplicity of wants and scarcity of resources
    (d) Shortage of labour.

31. Economics may be divided into macro-economics and micro economics. Among the subject matter of micro economics may be found

    (a) The nature of value in exchange
    (b) The size of country national income
    (c) Ther allocation of resources among competing uses
    (d) The relative prices of specific services.

32. The statement that "economics is positive and not normative" means

    (a) That ecnomics can be used to prove that capitalism is better than socialism
    (b) That economics tell us what kind of economic behaviour or policy is wholesome and what evil
    (c) The economic tell policy makers which alternative to choose from among several efficent ones
    (d) That economics can only indicate consequences of policies, choices or conditions.

33. Society faces economic problems because

    (a) Somebody invented money
    (b) Peoples wants are unlimited
    (c) Technology is not good enough
    (d) All of the above.

34. A function refers to
   (a) The demand for a commodity
   (b) The supply of a commodity
   (c) The demand and supply of a commodity
   (d) The relationship between one dependent variable and one or more independent variable.

35. The fact that economic goods and services are still scarce in every economy in the world means
   (a) That there are some economic wants that are not yet satisfied even though they may be pretty trovial wants by some standard
   (b) That it is necessary to ration economic goods and services since some wants must go unsatisfy
   (c) That our economic resources land, labour, capital etc. are also scarce
   (d) That our resources would be used in those ways in which their productivity is the greatest.

36. Economics
   (a) Contains a valid core of theory applicable to all
   (b) Economic system is normative
   (c) Is concerned only with capitalism
   (d) Predicts the near future but not the far future.

37. Economic laws may be described as
   (a) Principles derived from an analysis of prices and output determination
   (b) Generalisation concerning the economic behaviour of individual and institution
   (c) Forcasts of quantitative terms of the economic development of society
   (d) Expression of the basic feature of compitition.

38. There is no wealth but life wrote Ruskin. The economist uses the term *"wealth"* in a more restricted sense to mean
   (a) The cash and reserves held by a country's central banks and commercial banks

(b) The stock of goods existing at a given time and having money value

(c) Property owned by employer and amployees

(d) The store of goods capable of being used on more than one occasion.

39. If both meat and vegetable are economic goods for you this means

(a) That you have enough money to buy neither

(b) That you do not have enough money to buy either

(c) That they are for sale in your local market

(d) That you prefer to include more of both in your diet

(e) That they are not really scarce otherwise you could not get them.

40. Choice is fundamental to economic behaviour because

(a) People find it difficult to choose what they want

(b) Resources are scarce in relation to people wants

(c) Choosing make people act rationally

(d) Opportunity costs depend upon exercising choice

(e) prices depend on people making choices.

41. The main difference between positive economics and normative economics is that the former

(a) Discusses the ethical implications of its laws

(b) Concerns itself only with hypothesis which can generally be tested

(c) Is based on the value judgements of economists

(d) Considers carefully the political significance of its laws for a democratic society.

42. Micro economics deals primarily with

(a) Comparative statics, general equilibrium and positive economics

(b) Comparative statics, partial equilibrium and normative economics

(c) Dynamics, partial equilibrium and positive economics

(d) Comparative statics, partial equilibrium and positive economics.

43. A market
    (a) Necessarily refers to a meeting place between buyers and sellers where goods are bought and sold
    (b) Does not necessarily refer to a meeting place between buyers and sellers
    (c) Extends over the entire nation
    (d) Extends over a city.

44. Which one of the following is a normative statement or a question
    (a) Unemployment is a more serious social problem than inflation
    (b) What policies will reduce unemployment
    (c) An increases in government spending will reduce unemployment and increase inflation
    (d) What policies will prevent inflation.

45. If there were no scarcity of economic goods and services it would mean that
    (a) No one would want any economic goods and services
    (b) Economists would necessarily turn from the question of what kinds of output? to the question to whom will the output go?
    (c) There would be still be a number of wants unsatisfied but the definition these would not be very urgent wants
    (d) There would be no wants left unsatisfied at least no economic wants.

46. Robinson Crusoe is often quoted by economists as a simple model because
    (a) It is a story with which most people are familiar
    (b) The situation is completely different from the real world today
    (c) He did not need money
    (d) He had a essential basic economic problems to solve.

47. In order to get some sence of the urgency of people wants the most efficient system would be
    (a) To ask them simply to prepare the things they wanted

(b) To ask them prepare a list of things they wanted starting from the most urgent items and working down to the last urgent

(c) To ask them to prepare a list of the resources used in producing everything they wanted

(d) To give them a rationing system which would allow them to "spend" their ration points on whatever they wanted at set prices

(e) To tell them what their wants should be and use that as a appropciate list.

48. In a planned economy the economic problem of what shall be produced is determined primarily by

(a) Computers deciding what consumers wants

(b) Direction by the government

(c) The pattern of consumers spending

(d) The indepndent decisions of entrepreneurs.

49. The term "consumer goods" is used by economists to refer to

(a) Goods produced for consumers in a free market only

(b) Goods other than free goods whose use directly satisfies consumers wants

(c) Goods produced by consumers in turn for a wages

(d) Goods which are used by consumers in order to earn their living.

50. Assume that an economist is studying the textiles industries he would excluse from a consideration of the industry basic economic problem

(a) The price of wool

(b) The strength of textiles workers unions

(c) The financing of the various stages of textiles production

(d) The techniques of maintaining and repairing automated looms.

51. Which of the following is not an economic problem

(a) Deciding between extra paid work and extra leisure

(b) Deciding between different ways of spending leisure time
(c) Deciding not the level and form a personal saving
(d) Deciding between expenditure on one good and an other.

52. Which of the following statement is incorrect?
(a) Micro-economics is primarily concerned with the problem of what how and whom to produce
(b) Micro-economics is primarily concernd with the behaviour of individual decision making units when equilibrium
(c) Micro-economics is primarily concerend with time path and process by which one equilibrium evolves into another
(d) Micro-economics is primarily concerned with comparative statics rather than dynamics.

53. Which one of the following is not directly the concern of the economist
(a) Aid to underdeveloped countries
(b) The effect of an increase in bank rate
(c) The choice between alternative sites for a factory
(d) The use of taxation to discourage smoking of cigrettes.

54. Pick the odd statement:
(a) India's per capita income is relatively very low
(b) India's industrial output is relatively less than that in many industrialised developed countries like Denmark
(c) India's productivity of capital is low
(d) India's exports are miserably less than her import.

55. Mark the correct statement
(a) India is a stagnant economy
(b) India is underdeveloped economy
(c) India is developing economy
(d) India is a fast growing economy.

56. Pick out the incorrect statement of the following
    (a) Before Independence, foreign capital dominated all capital goods industries
    (b) Before Independence native capital and enterprise were interested only on jute and plantation industries
    (c) Foreign aid was flowing in uncontrolled dimension
    (d) All the above.

57. Which of the following statements is not correct?
    (a) Major investment during planning is in the public sector
    (b) The chief source of saving in Indian economy is the household sector
    (c) The gap between investment and domestic saving is filled through foreign saving
    (d) Public sector is not contributed to domestic saving.

58. Which of the following statement with regard to Indian railways is correct?
    (a) It is a commercial organisation
    (b) It is a public utility service
    (c) It is a private enterprise
    (d) All of them.

59. Which one of the following statements regarding the achievements is not correct?
    (a) The rate of interest is gross national product is markedly low
    (b) Per capita income is much less
    (c) Socialist pattern of economy is not properly adopted
    (d) Enormous black money is in circulation
    (e) Increase in exeports
    (f) Price rise has been checked since planning started.

60. Which of the following statements regarding fiscal and monetary system in India is not correct?
    (a) Regional rural banks in India are different from the commercial banks

(b) Finance Commission is appointed every 4 years by the president of India
(c) R.B.I is the only currency notes issuing agency
(d) R.B.I follow percentage system for issuing currency notes.

61. Which of the following factor is not responsible for low productivity in agriculture in India?
(a) Use of primitive equipment
(b) Financail weakness of the farmer
(c) Uneconomic size of holding
(d) Dependence on monsoon
(e) Lack of fertilizers.

62. Macth the following :

(1)	What is"	(I)	Micro-ecoomics
(2)	What ought to be"	(II)	Macro-economics
(3)	Aggregate	(III)	Positive economics
(4)	Individual units	(V)	Normative economics

	1	2	3	4
(a)	(iii)	(ii)	(iv)	(i)
(b)	(iii)	(iv)	(ii)	(i)
(c)	(iv)	(iii)	(i)	(ii)
(d)	(i)	(iv)	(iii)	(ii).

63. Match the following

(1)	Science of wealth	(i)	Marshall
(2)	Science of welfare	(ii)	Samuelson
(3)	Science dealing with scarcity	(iii)	Robbins
(4)	Science of growth	(iv)	Smith

	1	2	3	4
(a)	(ii),	(i)	(iii)	(iv)
(b)	(iv)	(ii)	(i)	(iii)
(c)	(iv)	(i)	(iii)	(ii)
(d)	(iii)	(ii)	(i)	(iv).

64. Bearing in mind the assertion that economics is a positive" and not a "normative" science with which of the following problems would an economist as economist be concerned?

(i) The unfairness of the distribution of wealth
(ii) The effect on prices of speculation in raw materials
(iii) The results of union pressure for increased wages
(iv) The rights and wrongs of exaggerated advertising claims.

65. The rights and wrongs of exaggerated advertising claims
(a) I only (b) Ii, iii,
.(c) I, iii (d) I, ii, iii, iv.

66. Which of the following is /are not matched correctly ?
i. First plan 1950-55 ii. Third plan 1961-66
iii. Fourth plan 1966-71 iv. Seventh plan 1985-90
(a) 1 and 2 (b) 3 only
(c) 1 only (d) 1 and 3.

67. Match the following columns?
(a) Depression (b) Recession
(c) Deflation (d) Stagflation.
i. Coexistence of inflation and stagnation
ii. Recovery from depression
iii. Reduction in production over a short period
iv. Insufficient demand leading to idle men and machinery over a long time
v. Reduction in level of economy due to following prices
(a) A-1, B-2, C-3, D-5 (b) A-4, B-3, C-2, D-5
(c) A-4, B-3, C-2, D-1 (d) A-3, B-4, C-2, D-1.

68. Which of the following is wrongly matched
(a) Cess—a compulsary levy collected by the government for a particular purpose from all persons.
(b) Rote—a compulsary levy collected by the government from the beneficiares of particular schemes
(c) Corporation—for levied by corporation for civic amenities
(d) Proportional tax— a tax levied at the same time at all levels of the base.

69. Match the following

Institution			year of formation
1.	National Stock Exchange	A.	1989
2.	OTDCE	B.	1992
3.	SEBI	C.	1993
4.	CARE	D.	1908.

(a) 1-A, 2-B, 3-C, 4-D, (b) 1-B, 2-A, 3-C, 4-D
(c) 1-B, 2-A, 3-D, 4-C (d) 1-C, 2-A, 3-D, 4-B.

70. Match the following

(a) Partial convertibility
(b) Convertibility on trade account
(c) Convertibility on current account
(d) Full convertibility.

1. Unified exchange rate applied for export and import of goods only i.e. visible transaction of BoP.
II. Currency can be converted on all accounts.
III. 60% of the foreign exchange to be converted at market rates and rest at official rate.
IV. Full convertibility in all visible and invisible trascation of goods and services.

(a) A-I, B-II, C-III, D-IV (b) A-III, B-I, C-IV, D-II
(c) A-IV, B-II, C-I, D-III (d) A-I, B-IV, C-III, D-II.

71. Which of the irrigation schemes and culturable command area fixed by the commission is/are matched wrongly?

I. Major— above 8,000 hectares
II. Medium— 2,000 to 10,000
III. Minor— less than 3,000

(a) 1 (b) 2
(c) 1& 2 (d) 1 &3.

72. Match the following:

1. Problem of resources allocation
(i) How to produce
2. Problem of choice of techniques
(ii) For whom to produce

3. Problem of distribution of
   (iii) What to produce
4. Problem of choice
   (iv) Security

	1	2	3	4
(a)	(iv)	(ii)	(i)	(iii)
(b)	(iii)	(i)	(ii)	(iv)
(c)	(iv)	(i)	(ii)	(iii)
(d)	(ii)	(i)	(iii)	(iv).

73. Which of the following conditions would relate to the concept of the "Perfect Market"?

I No preferential treatment
II Portability or transferability of the commoality
III A large number of buyers and sellers
IV Low prices at most times

(a) I, iii
(b) ii, iii,
(c) I, ii, iii
(d) I, ii, iii, iv.

CORRECT AND INCORRECT

74. Identify the factors responsible for the retarded economic development of India

I. long British rule II. shortage of capital
III. westrnised social attitude IV. caste system

(a) I and II (b) I, II, and III
(c) I, II, and IV (d) III and IV.

75. Which of the following features indicate that Indian economy is of the developing category?

I Occupation mainly agriculture
II Chronic unemployment
III Quality of human capital
IV Low Per Capita intake of proteins

(a) III (b) I, and IV
(c) II and III (d) I, II, III, and IV.

76. Which of the following one does not contribute to development of India ?
   (a) Technological research
   (b) Population growth
   (c) Diversification of Industry
   (d) Increased savings.

77. The National Development Council is mainly concerned with
   (a) Implementing state plan
   (b) approving and assessing major development project of India
   (c) Approval of five-year plans
   (d) Implementing community development programmes.

78. Since independence both development and non-development expenditure have increased the increase in the former being a little more than in the other non-development expenditure involves
   1. interest payments 2. subsidies
   3. defence 4. irrigation
   (a) 1 and 2
   (b) 1 only
   (c) 1, 2, and 3
   (d) 2, 3, and 4.

79. Developing economics are characterised by
   (a) Higher population growth rate
   (b) Higher dependence on import of manufactured goods
   (c) Higher land-man ratio
   (d) Higher ability to withstand seasonal fluctuation.

80. An important index of underdevelopment is
   (a) Low money national income
   (b) Low real national income
   (c) Low real per capita income
   (d) Low money per capita income.

81. In an underdeveloped economy the major contribution to the national product is made by
    (a) The primary sector
    (b) The secondary sector
    (c) The tertiary setor
    (d) Any of the above.

82. Disguised unemployment is a stable in which
    (a) More worker are engaged in a job than are required
    (b) A few worker make no contribution in the job in which they are engaged
    (c) The marginal product of labour is zero
    (d) Any of the above.

83. In a developed economy the major share of employment originates in the
    (a) Primary sector (b) Tertiary sector
    (c) Secondary sector (d) Any of the above.

84. As an economy develops
    (a) The share of Agricuture in nation products falls
    (b) The share of Agricuture in occupation structure falls
    (c) The shares of industry in national product rises
    (d) None of the above.

85. The Planning Commission of India
    I. was set up in 1950
    II. is a constitutional body
    III. is an advisory body
    IV. is a government department
    (a) I and II (b) II and III
    (c) I and III (d) III only.

86. The deputy chairman of the Planning Commission
    (a) Is the Prime Minister
    (b) Is the Planning Minister
    (c) Holds the rank of a cabinet minister
    (d) Is an economist of repute.

87. The basic objectives of Indian Planning are

I. economic growth

II. self reliance

III. employment generation

IV. population growth

(a) 1, 2, and 4 (b) 1, 2, and 3

(c) 2 and 3 (d) 1, 2, 3, and 4.

88. The best way to describe the over all aim of Indian Planning is

(a) Achievement of industrial development

(b) Growth and justice

(c) Socialism

(d) Regional prosperity.

89. Among the achievements of Indian planning we may include

I. development of strong infrastructure

II. diversification of industry and exports

III. high growth of national income

IV. strong control over prices

(a) 1 and 2 (b) 1, 2, and 3

(c) 1, 2, and 4 (d) 2 and 3.

90. The forth plan did not succeed because of

1. Indo-China conflict

2. Bangladesh refuge influx

3. Bad monsoon

4. Deteriorated prices situation

(a) 1, 3 and 4 (b) 1, 2 and 3

(c) 2, 3 and 4 (d) 1, 2, 3 and 4.

91. The emphasis in the Seventh Plan was on

(a) Education for all

(b) Food, work and productivity

(c) Removal of rural unemployment

(d) Decetralisation.

92. Which of the following were the priority objectives of the eighth plan ?

I. Universalisation of elementary education

II. Growth and diversification of agriculture

III. Containment of population growth

IV. Gradual privatisation of most public sector undertakings

(a) I, II and IV (b) II, III and IV

(c) I, III, and IV (d) I, II and III.

93. Which one of the following is the most important item of non-plan expenditure?

(a) Ex-interest payment

(b) Defence

(c) Fertilizer subsidies

(d) Loans to public enterprises.

94. Which of the following is not a non-planning expenditure

(a) Interest payment

(b) Subsidies

(c) Central assistance for state and UT plan

(d) Defence expenditure.

95. Indicative planning

(a) Replace of market- system

(b) Is a method of controlling the economy by settling short-term goals

(c) Can work and when capital accounts convertibility operates

(d) Works through the market.

96. Which of the following were the aims of the first five year plan?

(a) Starting a process of balanced all-round development of the economy

(b) Self-sufficiency in agriculture

(c) Building economic overhead

(d) All of these.

97. Which of the following were the specific objectives of the second five year plan?
    (a) Increase in national income
    (b) Rapid industrialisation with emphasis on heavy and basic industries
    (c) Expansion of employment opportunities
    (d) Better and more just distribution of income and wealth
    (e) All of these
    (f) Only (a) and (c).

98. Which one of the following was not the objective of third five year plan?
    (a) Raising national income by 8 % per annum
    (b) Achieving self-sufficiency in foodgrains
    (c) Expand basic and key industries
    (d) Utilities manpower resources
    (e) Spreading literacy.

99. Which one of the following were the objectives of fourth five year plan?
    (a) Promoting growth with suitability
    (b) Better utilisation of domestic resources
    (c) Creating regional imbalances
    (d) Correcting regional imbalances
    (e) All of these
    (f) Only (b) and (c).

100. Which one of the following was not the domestic sources for financing the five year plan?
    (a) Taxation
    (b) Public borrowing
    (c) Domestic saving
    (d) Voluntary contributions from big industrial houses.

101. The Planning Commision of India is
    (a) A constitutional body as the Supreme Court
    (b) A non-statutory body created by the centre

(c) A statutory body entrusted with all economic planning in India

(d) An independent and autonomous body performing advisory and research functions to help the government of India.

102. By financing of the plan we mean

(a) Raising financial resources to execute to physical targets

(b) Reducing the size

(c) Reducing the size of the plan to bring it in line with the available resources.

103. The growth of the Indian economy during the first three decades of planning was not commensurate with the rising levels of investment primarily because of

(a) Falling savings in the economy

(b) Rising price level in the economy

(c) Expanding money supply in the economy

(d) Increasing capital-output ratio.

104. During the Seventh Plan the contribution of the agricultural sector to the G.D.P.

(a) Was less than that of the tertiary sector

(b) Was less than that of the secondary sector

(c) Increased proportionately over the corresponding period during the sixth plan

(d) Was the highest among the three sectors.

105. At the threshold of the Eighth Plan

(a) Population growth has halted in the Indian economy

(b) Incidence of infant mortality has come down significantly

(c) The gap between growth of labour force and growth of employment is widening

(d) Inflation is no more a problem.

106. Critical imbalances in the Indian economy on the eve of the eighth plan can be identified as

(a) Increasing fiscal and budgetary deficits

(b) Critical situation in the balance of payments

(c) High rate of inflation
(d) All of the above.

107. During the seventh plan balances from current revenues and contribution of public enterprises, both inclusive of additional resource mobilisation, were to finance about
(a) 10 per cent of the total public sector investment
(b) 20 per cent of the total public sector investment
(c) 30 per cent of the total public sector investment
(d) 40 per cent of the total public sector investment.

108. During the seventh plan, balances from current revenues and contribution of public enterprises, both inclusive of additional resource mobilisation, finance
(a) 10 per cent of the total public sector investment
(b) 20 per cent of the total public sector investment
(c) 30 per cent of the total public sector investment
(d) 40 per cent of the total public sector investment.

109. The public sector investment of the order envisaged in the eighth plan requires that the
(a) Dissolving of the government must rise steeply
(b) Dissolving of the government must come down sharply
(c) Dissolving of the government remains unchanged
(d) Dissolving of the government need not be considered.

110. The Eighth Plan has a focus among which the following is not included
(a) Clear priorisation of sectors for investment
(b) Creating a social security net through employment generation
(c) Creation of appropriate delivery systems to ensure the benefit of invest beneficiaries
(d) Achievement of self-sufficiency in industrial production.

111. Among the objectives laid down before the eighth plan the following is not mentioned
(a) Universalisation of elementary education

(b) Provision of safe drinking water and primary wealth are the facilities
(c) Incentives for better education and larger size of families
(d) Generation of adequate employment.

112. In the eighth plan it has been recommended that the consideration of holdings should be made compulsory in
(a) All the states
(b) The high-growth regions
(c) The command of the large irrigation projects
(d) The north-eastern districts.

113. The strategy for agricultural development in the eighth plan aims at
(a) Achieving self-sufficiency in food
(b) Generating surpluses of specific agricultural commodities for export
(c) Shifting the land area from cultivation of food crops to the cultivation of crops meant for export.

114. In almost all the sectors of the economy during the eighth plan it is estimated that there
(a) Will be a shift from the private sector to the public sector
(b) Will be a shift from the public to the private sector
(c) Will be a shift from the private sector to the point sector.

115. The financing pattern of the eighth plan public sector outway stipulates
(a) Reduced share of market borrowings
(b) Increased share of miscellaneous capital receipts
(c) increased rate of personal income taxation.

116. During the seventh plan the contribution of PSE's and their resource mobilisation through issue of bonds etc. amount for about
(a) 16.2 per cent of the total expenditure
(b) 18.2 per cent of the total expenditure

(c) 19.2 per cent of the total expenditure
(d) 21.2 per cent of the total expenditure.

117. On which of the following basis the Planning Commission has defined poverty in India?
(a) Nutritional requirement of 2400 calories per person per day for urban areas
(b) Nutritional requirement of 2100 calories per person per day for rural areas
(c) Neither of these
(d) Both of these.

118. The Eighth Plan emphasise in particular the need for
(i) Continued reliance on domestic resource for financing investment
(ii) Increasing the technical capabilities for the develoment of science and technology
(iii) Modernisation and competitive efficiency
(iv) Reduction in inequalities of income
(a) (i) (b) (i) + (ii)
(c) (i) + (ii) + (iii) (d) (i) + (ii) + (iii) + (iv).

ANSWERS

1.	(c)	2.	(b)	3.	(a)	4.	(b)
5.	(d)	6.	(b)	7.	(c)	8.	(d)
9.	(a)	10.	(b)	11.	(a)	12.	(a)
13.	(b)	14.	(a)	15.	(c)	16.	(a)
17.	(b)	18.	(c)	19.	(d)	20.	(d)
21.	(c)	22.	(c)	23.	(a)	24.	(b)
25.	(d)	26.	(b)	27.	(c)	28.	(c)
29.	(d)	30.	(c)	31.	(c)	32.	(d)
33.	(b)	34.	(d)	35.	(e)	36.	(a)
37.	(b)	38.	(b)	39.	(d)	40.	(b)
41.	(b)	42.	(d)	43.	(a)	44.	(a)
45.	(d)	46.	(d)	47.	(d)	48.	(b)
49.	(b)	50.	(d)	51.	(b)	52.	(c)
53.	(d)	54.	(b)	55.	(d)	56.	(d)
57.	(d)	58.	(c)	59.	(f)	60.	(d)

61.	(e)	62.	(b)	63.	(c)	64.	(b)
65.	(d)	66.	(b)	67.	(c)	68.	(c)
69.	(c)	70.	(b)	71.	(d)	72.	(c)
73.	(c)	74.	(c)	75.	(d)	76.	(b)
77.	(c)	78.	(c)	79.	(a)	80.	(c)
81.	(a)	82.	(d)	83.	(b)	84.	(d)
85.	(c)	86.	(c)	87.	(b)	88.	(b)
89.	(a)	90.	(c)	91.	(b)	92.	(d)
93.	(a)	94.	(c)	95.	(b)	96.	(d)
97.	(e)	98.	(e)	99.	(e)	100.	(d)
101.	(b)	102.	(a)	103.	(d)	104.	(a)
105.	(c)	106.	(d)	107.	(d)	108.	(b)
109.	(b)	110.	(d)	111.	(c)	112.	(c)
113.	(d)	114.	(a)	115.	(d)	116.	(d)
117.	(d)	118.	(e)				

2
POVERTY AND INEQUALITY

1. On which of the following basis the Planning Commission has defined poverty in India ?
   (a) Nutritional requirement of 2400 calories per person per day for urban areas
   (b) Nutritional requirement of 2100 calories per person per day for rural areas
   (c) Neither of these
   (d) Both of these.

2. Which of the following is not the economic factor for the causes of poverty?
   (a) Fast rise in population
   (b) Low productivity in agriculture
   (c) Inequalities of income
   (d) Mass illiteracy.

3. Which of the following measures cannot remove poverty ?
   (a) Population control
   (b) Government subsidies
   (c) Increase in production
   (d) Equitable distribution.

4. The inequalities of income in the non-agricultural sector area ?
   (a) Increasing (b) Decreasing
   (c) Stable (d) All of these.

5. Which of the following are the causes of inequalities of income ?
   (a) The institution of private property
   (b) The law of inequality
   (c) Economic exploitation
   (d) All of these.

6. Which is not the effect of the inequalities of income?
   (a) Unemployment
   (b) Concentration of economic power
   (c) Difference in standard of living
   (d) Depression in industries.

7. In the seventh plan the poverty line in urban areas has been fixed at
   (a) Rs. 107 (b) Rs. 112
   (c) Rs. 117 (d) Rs. 122.

8. In the seventh plan the poverty line in rural areas has been fixed at an income level of Rs. 107. This is at the price level in the year.
   (a) 1979-80 (b) 1984-85
   (c) 1985-86 (d) 1989-90.

9. The percentage of population below the poverty line targeted for the terminated year of the seventh plan is
   (a) 16.8 per cent
   (b) 25.8 per cent
   (c) 17.5 per cent
   (d) 10.8 per cent.

10. Which of the following is not one of the main aim of land reform ?
    (a) To take more rational use of the scare land resource
    (b) State control of the means of production
    (c) To redistribute agricultural land in favour to the less privileged class
    (d) To improve the terms and conditions on which land is held for cultivation by actual tillers.

11. Which of the following is a direct method to reduce economic inequalities?
(a) Estate duty (b) Wealth tax
(c) Capital gaining tax (d) Ceiling on holdings.

12. The percentage of the Indian rural population below the poverty line for 1984 - 85 was
(a) 30.09 (b) 40.62
(c) 45.72 (d) 39.90.

13. One of the following is not a cause of poverty in India - which?
(a) Abundant population
(b) Abundant natural resources
(c) Abundant inequalities in distribution of income
(d) Abundant of surplus manpower in agriculture.

14. The most important remedy to the problem of poverty in India is
(a) Changes in the ownership pattern
(b) Higher productivity
(c) Redistribution or income through fiscal, pricing and other measures
(d) All of the above.

15. For urban areas poverty line has been determined at 1979-80 prices at the income level
(a) Rs. 76 per month
(b) Rs. 107 per month
(c) Rs. 122 per month
(d) Rs. 98 per month.

16. The economist who warned against population explosion is
(a) Alfred Marshall (b) Karl Marx
(c) Malthus (d) None of the above.

17. Which is the least densely populated state of India?
(a) Rajasthan (b) Nagaland
(c) Gujarat (d) M.P.

18. For rural areas poverty line has been determined 1984-85 prices at the income level of:
    (a) Rs. 76 per month (b) Rs. 107 per month
    (c) Rs. 122 per month (d) Rs. 96 per month.

19. According to the Seventh Plan 1985-90, the number of people living below the poverty line in rural area is
    (a) 41 per cent (b) 48 per cent
    (c) 53 per cent (d) 54 per cent.

20. The celebrated book "the Challenge of World Poverty" has been written by
    (a) Galbraith (b) Kindleberger
    (c) G. Myrdal (d) Dadabhai Naoroji.

21. In urban areas at 1984 - 85 prices the Planning Commission in the seventh plan 1985-90 has defined the poverty line at
    (a) Rs. 65.00 (b) Rs. 122.00
    (c) Rs. 73.50 (d) Rs. 77.20.

22. A substantial segment of a society is deprived when it lags
    (a) The minimum necessities
    (b) The minimum level of living
    (c) Comforts and luxuries
    (d) None of the above.

23. Large percentage of the population in the age group 0-14 years indicate the presence of
    (a) Unproductive consumer
    (b) Working force
    (c) High death rate
    (d) Low birth rate.

24. The study group set up by the Planning Commission in 1962 had recommended (at 1960-61 prices)
    (a) Rs. 20 per capita per month as bare minimum
    (b) Rs. 25 per capita per month as bare minimum
    (c) Rs. 30 per capita per month as bare minimum
    (d) None of the above.

25. The poverty line according to the alternative definition of the Planning Commission, is at least to have a daily calorie intake of per person in rural areas and in urban areas.

(a) 18000, 1700
(b) 2,400, 2100
(c) 2900, 2000
(d) 2500, 2100.

26. The incidence of poverty can be computed from

(a) NAS data on national accounts
(b) NSS data on consumption of expenditure
(c) Both (a) and (b)
(d) None of the above.

27. On the basis of calorie intake the minimum income in 1979-80 prices term out to be Rs. — for

(a) 88, 75 (b) 82, 90
(c) 76, 88 (d) 75, 89.

28. The seventh plan estimates of the incidence of poverty were for the year

(a) 1983-84 (b) 1984- 85
(c) 1985-86 (d) 1986- 87.

29. According to the seventh plan document --------% of the rural population were below the poverty line in 1983-84 .

(a) 43.2 (b) 42.2
(c) 41.2 (d) 40.2.

30. In 1983-84 the percentage of urban population below the poverty line was

(a) 28.1 (b) 30.1
(c) 32.1 (d) 34.1.

31. All estimates of the incidence of poverty line based on

(a) Family count
(b) Head count
(c) (a) and (b)
(d) None of the above.

32. In India the study of poverty were made by
   (a) Dandekar & Rath
   (b) P.K. Bardhan & B.S. Minhas
   (c) Dandekar, P.K. Bardhan, B.S. Minhas & M.S. Ahluwalia
   (d) I.J. Ahluwalia.

33. The seventh plan aimed at reducing the percentage of population below poverty line to ———% by 1990.
   (a) 35.2 (b) 33.2
   (c) 30.2 (d) 28.2.

34. Which of the following measures cannot remove poverty ?
   (a) Increase in population
   (b) Increase in growth subsidy
   (c) Equal distribution of income and wealth
   (d) Population control.

35. The inequalities of income in the urban areas are
   (a) Increasing
   (b) Decreasing
   (c) Stable
   (d) All the above.

36. Which of the following are the causes of the inequalities in income and distribution ?
   (a) The law of inheritance
   (b) The institution of private property
   (c) Economic exploitation
   (d) All the above.

37. What measure was suggested by Karl Marx for the reduction of inequality of income
   (a) Equal income for all
   (b) Income according to needs
   (c) Higher tax on unearned income
   (d) Increasing the income of the poor.

38. Which of the following is not a poverty alleviation programme ?
    (a) Small Farmers Development Agency
    (b) Drought prone A programme
    (c) Special foodgrain production programme
    (d) Food for Work programme.

39. The rate of growth of population has been highest during the decade
    (a) 1900 -11 (b) 1921-31
    (c) 1951-61 (d) 1961-71.

40. The density of the Union Territory of Delhi is approximately
    (a) 1200 (b) 2200
    (c) 3200 (d) 4200.

41. The approximate percentage of population that lives in village is
    (a) 50 (b) 60
    (c) 70 (d) 76.

42. The birth rate increasing the number of births during a year per
    (a) 100 of population (b) 1000 of population
    (c) Million of population (d) None of the above.

43. Density of population indicates the
    (a) Capital-land ratio (b) Land-output ratio
    (c) Land-labour ratio (d) Man-land ratio.

44. According to the seventh plan document the death rate in 1990 was
    (a) 6.4 (b) 10.4
    (c) 14.4 (d) 18.4.

45. The highest rate of growth of population for India had been recorded for
    (a) The 1941-51 decade (b) The 1951-61 decade
    (c) The 1961-71 decade (d) The 1971-81 decade.

46. The total population of scheduled castes and scheduled tribes in India according to 1981 census is nearly per cent

(a) 17.5% (b) 20.5%
(c) 23.5% (d) 25.5%.

47. Because of absolute increase in India's rural population we can say

(a) India is getting more rural
(b) India is getting urbanised at a fast speed
(c) India is getting urbanised at low speed
(d) None of the above.

48. The normal reproductive age group among the farmers in India is between

(a) 14 to 35 years (b) 16 to 40 years
(c) 14 to 44 years (d) 18 to 52 years.

49. Universal Immunisation Programme for infants is and expectant mothers was started in India

(a) 1975-76 (b) 1977-78
(c) 1980-81 (d) 1985-86.

50. The family planning programme was officially launched in India for the first time in

(a) 1950 (b) 1952
(c) 1955 (d) 1956.

51. The percentage distribution of the age composition of Indian population show the highest population to be in the age group

(a) 0-14 years (b) 15-60 years
(c) 60 and over (d) 0-9 years.

52. What is the approximate density of population in India ?

(a) 516 (b) 416
(c) 316 (d) 216.

53. Objective of removal of poverty and attainment of economic self-reliance ?

(a) Second (b) Third
(c) Fourth (d) Fifth.

54. The total amount to be spent on the family planning programme during the sixth plan was approximately in Rs —— crores

(a) 1,000 (b) 2200
(c) 4400 (d) 8800.

55. In the 7th plan the poverty line in urban areas has been fixed at

(a) Rs. 122 (b) Rs. 166
(c) Rs. 144 (d) Rs. 227.

56. Which one of the following Union Territories has the highest rate ?

(a) 1990 AD (b) 1995 AD
(c) 2000 AD (d) 2005 AD.

57. The new education policy was announced by government of India in

(a) 1982 (b) 1984
(c) 1986 (d) 1988.

58. According to the seventh plan document the death rate in 1990 was

(a) 6.4 (b) 10.4
(c) 14.4 (d) 18.4.

59. Which of the following state has a highest growth rate in population ?

(a) Bihar (b) Uttar Pradesh
(c) Nagaland (d) West Bengal.

60. The actual population in India as on March 1991 is

(a) 843.92 million
(b) 842.51 million
(c) 843.11 million
(d) 844.09 million.

61. The number of female to male per thousand is computed at

(a) 928 (b) 929
(c) 930 (d) 931.

62. Which of the following states has the highest density of population according to 1991 census ?
    (a) Uttar Pradesh
    (b) West Bengal
    (c) Maharashtra
    (d) Andhra Pradesh.

63. Which of the following states recorded a lowest growth rate in population ?
    (a) Tamil Nadu (b) Karnataka
    (c) Goa (d) Kerala.

64. Population in the 80's represent a percent rise over the population in the 70's
    (a) 21.5 (b) 22.5
    (c) 23.5 (d) 24.5.

65. The rational population policy was announced in years
    (a) 1975 (b) 1976
    (c) 1977 (d) 1978.

66. A full-fledged department of family planning was set in the year
    (a) 1963 (b) 1964
    (c) 1965 (d) 1966.

67. The Planning Commission envisaged a reduction in non reduction rate to 1 as a whole by
    (a) 1995 (b) 1996
    (c) 1997 (d) 1998.

68. The objective of family planning programme is to bring down the birth rate to
    (a) 22 per cent (b) 23 p.c.
    (c) 24 p.c. (d) 25 p.c.

69. In spite of no decline in population growth the rate of domestic saving fluctuated around
    (a) 15 % (b) 14 %
    (c) 13% (d) 12%.

70. According to R. Cassen's view that the growth of population output per worker
    (a) Also increases
    (b) Does not increase
    (c) Remain constant
    (d) Remains stagnant.

71. According to the 1991 census the density of population in India was
    (a) 260 per Sq. Km (b) 259 per Sq. Km.
    (c) 258 per Sq. Km (d) 257 per Sq. Km.

72. In India the presence of population on land has been
    (a) Steadily declining
    (b) Seadily increasing
    (c) Constant over the planning period
    (d) Negligible.

ANSWERS

1.	(d)	2.	(d)	3.	(b)	4.	(d)
5.	(a)	6.	(d)	7.	(d)	8.	(b)
9.	(b)	10.	(b)	11.	(d)	12.	(d)
13.	(d)	14.	(d)	15.	(d)	16.	(c)
17.	(b)	18.	(b)	19.	(a)	20.	(c)
21.	(b)	22.	(b)	23.	(b)	24.	(a)
25.	(b)	26.	(b)	27.	(a)	28.	(a)
29.	(d)	30.	(a)	31.	(b)	32	(c)
33.	(a)	34.	(b)	35.	(a)	36.	(d)
37.	(b)	38.	(a)	39.	(d)	40.	(d)
41.	(b)	42.	(b)	43.	(d)	44.	(b)
45.	(d)	46.	(c)	47.	(c)	48.	(c)
49.	(d)	50.	(b)	51.	(b)	52.	(d)
53.	(d)	54.	(a)	55.	(a)	56.	(b)
57.	(c)	58.	(b)	59.	(c)	60.	(a)
61.	(b)	62.	(d)	63.	(c)	64.	(c)
65.	(b)	66.	(d)	67.	(b)	68.	(d)
69.	(d)	70.	(a)	71.	(d)	72.	(b)

3
PLANNING IN INDIA

1. Planning in India had been started from the year
   (a) 1947 (b) 1949
   (c) 1950 (d) 1951.
2. During the first five year plan, national income rose at the rate of
   (a) 2 % per annum (b) 3 % per annum
   (c) 3.5 % per annum (d) 3.6 % per annum.
3. The first five year plan was based on
   (a) Sorrow model
   (b) Mahalanobis
   (c) Hammod - Domar model
   (d) Samuelson model.
4. During the first five year plan, the per capita income of India grown at the rate of
   (a) 0.9 % per annum (b) 1.7 % per annum
   (c) 1.5 % per annum (d) 1.6 % per annum.
5. The second five year plan accorded top priority to
   (a) Industry (b) Agriculture
   (c) Land-reform (d) Inter.
6. The second five year plan was on
   (a) Harrod-Domare model
   (b) Vakil- Bramhanand model
   (c) Mahalanobis model
   (d) Saloro model.

7. The share of 'Industry and minerals' in the second plan rate to
   (a) 20% of total expenditure
   (b) 20.1 % of total expenditure
   (c) 20.2 % of total expenditure
   (d) 19.8 % of total expenditure.

8. The minimum need programme was initiated in the
   (a) First plan (b) Third plan
   (c) Fifth plan (d) Seventh plan.

9. The second plan aimed at increasing the national income at compound annual rate of
   (a) 4.5 % (b) 4.6%
   (c) 4.7% (d) 5%.

10. The target for increase in national income in the third five year plan was
   (a) 5.5 % per annum (b) 5.6 % per annum
   (c) 6% per annum (d) 6.1 % per annum.

11. What was the total outlay at the third plan?
   (a) Rs. 4, 672 crores (b) 5.6% per annum
   (c) 6% per annum (d).

12. India's fourth five year plan covered the period
   (a) 1961-1966 (b) 1966-71
   (c) 1969-1974 (d) 1970-1975.

13. The target of annual rate of growth was not realized in most of the plans, except
   (a) First and the third plan
   (b) Second and the sixth plan
   (c) Third and the fourth plan
   (d) First and the sixth plan.

14. The rural unemployment programmes such as NREP and RLEGP were introduced in the
   (a) First plan (b) Third plan
   (c) Fifth plan (d) Sixth plan.

15. India's fifth five year plan covered the period
    (a) 1975-1980 (b) 1974-1979
    (c) 1976-1981 (d) 1977-1981.

16. What was the total outlay of the fourth plan?
    (a) Rs. 15, 770 crores (b) Rs 15, 777 crores
    (c) Rs. 15, 779 crores (d) Rs. 15, 800 crores.

17. The seventh five year plan came into operation from
    (a) 1 st April 1984 (b) 30 th March 1985
    (c) 1 st April 1985 (d) 1 st May 1985.

18. The seventh plan's targeted growth GDP was
    (a) 4.5% per annum (b) 5% per annum
    (c) 5.5 % per annum (d) 5.6% per annum.

19. The rate of gross domestic capital formation in the seventh plan was projected to a rise of
    (a) 24.6 % (b) 25%
    (c) 25.9% (d) 26%.

20. The total plan outlay for public sector in seventh plan was
    (a) Rs. 1,79,000 crores (b) Rs. 1,80,000 crores
    (c) Rs. 1,85,000 crores (d) Rs, 1,86,000 crores.

21. The real increased saving rate during the seventh plan was
    (a) 20.4% (b) 20.6 %
    (c) 21% (d) 21.2%.

22. In the seventh plan the target share in the allocation of fund went to
    (a) Agriculture (b) Rural development
    (c) Energy (d) Science and Technology.

23. According to the provisional estimates deficit financing for the seventh plan actually amounted to
    (a) Rs. 34,126 crores (b) Rs. 35,291 crores
    (c) Rs. 36,000 crores (d) Rs. 36,126 crores.

24. The actual deficit during the fifth plan amounted to
    (a) Rs. 1, 354 crores (b) Rs. 2, 290 crores
    (c) Rs. 3, 560 crores (d) Rs. 3, 590 crores.

25. In India long term planning was suspended between
    (a) 1966 and 1969 (b) 1965 and 1968
    (c) 1964 and 1967 (d) 1967 and 1970.

26. During the seventh plan period GDP rose at the rate of
    (a) 5% per annum (b) 5.5 % per annum
    (c) 5.6 % per annum (d) 5.7 % per annum.

27. The realised growth rate of the agricultural sector in the seventh plan was
    (a) 3.2 % per annum (b) 3.4 % per annum
    (c) 3.5 % per annum (d) 3.6 % per annum.

28. During the seventh plan period the realised growth rate in the manufacturing sector was
    (a) 7.5 % per annum (b) 7.7 % per annum
    (c) 7.9 % per annum (d) 8% per annum.

29. The eighth five year plan has been commenced from
    (a) 31 st March 1990 (b) 1 st April 1990
    (c) 1 st April 1991 (d) 1 st April 1992.

30. What is the projected growth rate during the eighth plan?
    (a) 6% (b) 5.6 %
    (c) 5.5 % (d) 5%.

31. During the eighth plan period exports will grow at
    (a) 12 % of GDP (b) 13 % of GDP
    (c) 13.6 % of GDP (d) 14 % of GDP.

32. During the eight plan period imports will be restricted at
    (a) 8.4 % of GDP (b) 8% of GDP
    (c) 8.5 % of GDP (d) 9% of GDP.

33. What is the postulated size of the Eighth Plan?
    (a) Rs. 7,95,000 crores (b) Rs. 7,98,000 crores
    (c) Rs. 8,00,000 crores (d) Rs. 8,10,000 crores.

34. In percentage terms what was the allocation to 'agriculture and allied sector in the first plan?

(a) 14.3 (b) 14.4

(c) 14.6 (d) 14.8.

35. The 'agriculture and allied' sector in the second plan was

(a) 11.3% (b) 11.5%

(c) 11.7 % (d) 11.9%.

36. The seventh plan aimed at bringing down the poverty ratio to

(a) 25.8 % (b) 30.1%

(c) 32 % (d) 34.9%.

37. During the seventh plan electricity generation realised an increase at the rate of

(a) 9.1% per annum

(b) 9.2% per annum

(c) 9.3 % per annum

(d) 9.4 % per annum.

38. In the seventh plan period the services sector registered 6.5 % per annum increase in the

(a) Gross output

(b) Net output

(c) Net output at the sector cost

(d) Gross out put at the factor cost.

39. In the Seventh Plan period the highest rate of growth has been realised in the

(a) Metal-based products

(b) Capital goods sector

(c) Consumer durable goods sector

(d) Petroleum products.

40. The Government of India's internal debt-GDP ratio is presently close to

(a) 40% (b) 50%

(c) 50.2% (d) 51.9%.

41. In the terminal year of the Seventh Plan the ratio of the external debt to NNP was

(a) 23 % (b) 22.9%
(c) 21.7% (d) 21.6%.

42. In 1989-90 India's long term debt services ratio to GNP was

(a) 2.2 % (b) 2.3%
(c) 2.4% (d) 2.5%.

43. In 1991-92 the fiscal deficit was brought down to

(a) 7 % of G.D.P (b) 6.5 % of G.D.P
(c) 6 % of G.D.P (d) 5 % of G.D.P.

44. In the budget proposal of 1991-92 average price of fertiliser has been increased by

(a) 25 % (b) 28 %
(c) 30 % (d) 31 %.

45. The largest singular item of non-plan expenditure is

(a) Subsidy on social services
(b) Subsidy on education
(c) Government's non development expenditure
(d) Interest rate changes.

46. During the past two decades, employment has grown at the rate of

(a) 1.5% per annum (b) 2 % per annum
(c) 2.2 % per annum (d) 2.5 % per annum.

47. Planning for an expanding economy was written by

(a) C.N Vakil and P.R Bramhanand
(b) J. Bhagwati and S. Chakravorty
(c) Promod Bardhan
(d) Ashok Mitra.

48. The wage-good strategy of development was formulated by

(a) Amartya Sen
(b) C.N Vakil and P.R Bramhanand
(c) P.C. Mahalanobis
(d) J. Bhagwati.

49. The wage good is the wage-good strategy consist exclusively of

(a) Consumer durables (b) Capital goods

(c) Food (d) Electronic products.

50. The two stratgic objectives of the fifth plan were

(a) Removal of poverty and self-reliance

(b) Industrialization productivity

(c) Modernisation and scientific innovation

(d) Commercialization and marketable surplus.

51. National Planning Committee under the chairmanship of Pandit Jawahar Lal Nehru was set up in the year

(a) 1937 (b) 1938

(c) 1947 (d) 1948.

52. The proposed planning period of the 'Bombay Plan' (1944) was

(a) 10 years (b) 5 years

(c) 15 years (d) 20 years.

53. The Bombay Plan (1944) envisaged an expenditure of

(a) Rs. 11,000 crores

(b) Rs. 10,000 crores

(c) Rs. 9,000 crores

(d) Rs. 8,500 crores.

54. Almost simultaneously with the 'Bombay Plan' the 'people plan' was charted by

(a) P.C. Joshi (b) M.N. Roy

(c) B.T. Randive (d) Jyoti Basu.

55. The first industrial policy of the Government of India announced in the year

(a) 1947 (b) 1948

(c) 1949 (d) 1951.

56. Planning Commission in India was set up in the year

(a) 1947 (b) 1949

(c) 1950 (d) 1951.

57. Who wrote the book "*Development Planning: the Indian Experience*"?
    (a) Amartya Sen
    (b) Pranab Bardhan
    (c) Kaushik Basu
    (d) Sukhomoy Chakravarty.

58. The pioneering book on planning in India entitled "Planned Economy for India" was authored by
    (a) P.S. Lokanathan (b) V. K. R .V. Rao
    (c) M. Visvesvaraya (d) C. W. Vakil.

59. Indian planning
    (a) Is totalitarian in nature (b) Is democratic in nature
    (c) Is totally centralised (d) Is none of the above.

60. The most important domestic source of financing plans is
    (a) Domestic saving
    (b) Surplus from current revenues
    (c) Public loans
    (d) All of the above.

61. The famous Gandhian plan was prepared by
    (a) M.N. Roy (b) Sriman Narayan
    (c) D.P. Dhar (d) C. Subramaniam.

62. Mahalanobis model laid great emphasis on the development of
    (a) Agriculture
    (b) Heavy industries
    (c) Energy
    (d) Science and technology.

63. Self-reliance as an aspect of planning was emphasised first in
    (a) Second five year plan
    (b) Third five year plan
    (c) Fourth five year plan
    (d) Fifth five year plan.

64. The original approach paper of the fifth five year plan was prepared under
    (a) C. Subramaniam (b) K.C. Neyogi
    (c) V.K.R.V. Rao (d) D.P. Dhar.

65. A five year plan is a
    (a) Medium term plan (b) Perspective plan
    (c) Short term plan (d) None of these.

66. The fifth five year plan of India terminated on
    (a) 31 March 1971 (b) 31 March 1975
    (c) 31 March 1976 (d) 31 March 1978.

67. In the seventh plan the share of public sector in the total investment was
    (a) 46 % (b) 46.8 %
    (c) 49.8 % (d) 47.5 %.

68. In which of the plan, India's growth of agricultural product was negative
    (a) Second plan (b) Third plan
    (c) Fourth plan (d) Fifth plan.

69. A perspective plan converts a time horizon of
    (a) 1 to 2 years (b) 5 years
    (c) 15 to 20 years (d) None of the above.

70. The minimum need programme was introduced in India in the
    (a) Third plan (b) Fourth plan
    (c) Fifth plan (d) Sixth plan.

71. Removal of poverty and unemployment have been spelt out explicitly in the
    (a) First plan (b) Second plan
    (c) Fourth plan (d) Sixth plan.

72. The seventh plan envisaged an annual growth rate per capita income of the order of
    (a) 2 per cent (b) 3 per cent
    (c) 4 per cent (d) 4.5 per cent.

73. The major emphasis in the Third Plan was on
   (a) Making India self-reliant
   (b) Adult Education
   (c) Green Revolution
   (d) Food for Work Programme.

74. By the end of seventh plan, poverty ratio was expected to go down to
   (a) 36.9 per cent (b) 48.6 per cent
   (c) 25.8 per cent (d) 10.0 per cent.

75. Total outlay (both public sector and private sector) taken together on the seventh plan was envisaged at
   (a) Rs. 1,80,000 crores
   (b) Rs. 3,22,366 crores
   (c) Rs. 3,48,148 crores
   (d) Rs. 1,54,218 crores.

76. Total domestic resources as a percentage of total seventh plan public sector outlay worked out at
   (a) 85 per cent (b) 90 per cent
   (c) 94 per cent (d) 96 per cent.

77. In Seventh Plan the share of private sector in the total plan outlay was
   (a) 48.7% (b) 49.6%
   (c) 51% (d) 52.2%.

78. Who finally approves the five year plan?
   (a) Parliament and state legislatures
   (b) National Development Council
   (c) Planning Commission
   (d) The President.

79. In eighth plan the share of private sector and public sector in the total plan outlay is respectively
   (a) 55% and 45% (b) 54.8% and 45.2%
   (c) 52% and 48% (d) 53.7% and 46.3%.

80. Largest proportion of public sector outlay in the seventh plan was allocated to
   (a) Agriculture and rural development
   (b) Industry and minerals
   (c) Energy
   (d) Transport.

81. In India's five year plans greater reliance for financing has been placed on
   (a) Contribution of net inflow from foreign country
   (b) Return on our investment in foreign country
   (c) Remittances by Indians abroad
   (d) Domestic resource.

82. By financing of plan we mean
   (a) Raising financial resources to execute programme incorporated in a plan
   (b) Matching financial resources to physical target
   (c) Reducing the size of the plan to bring it within the available resources
   (d) Implementation and realisation of the plan targets.

83. The seventh plan strategy was built around
   (a) Greatest emphasis on agriculture only
   (b) Food, work and productivity
   (c) Rapid growth of industries only
   (d) Minimum need programme.

84. External assistance as a source of financing of outlay in the public sector was highest in the third plan. It amounted to
   (a) 36.2 per cent of total financial outlay
   (b) 26.4 per cent of total financial outlay
   (c) 26.4 per cent of total financial outlay
   (d) 28.3 per cent of total financial outlay.

85. The Mahalanobis planning model on which the second plan strategy was based is essentially
   (a) A two sector consistency model
   (b) A linear programming model

(c) An optimizing model
(d) An optimizing model of Thorndike type.

86. The long term financial policy formulated in the context of the seventh five year plan lays emphasis on
(a) Tackling the problem of poverty and unemployment
(b) Reforming Tax system
(c) Capital formation by increasing money income and reducing consumption
(d) Making taxes easily comprehensible to the tax payers.

87. "Growth was stable" and progressive achievement of "self-reliance" were the basic objectives of
(a) Second five year plan
(b) Third five year plan
(c) Fourth five year plan
(d) Fifth five year plan.

88. The objectives of social justice articulated in our plans has two major dimensions
(a) Improvement is overall living standards and better employment opportunities
(b) Amelioration of the condition of farm labourers and eradication
(c) Improvement in the living standard of the poorest group and reduction in inequalities in asset ownership
(d) None of them.

89. Deficit financing means
(a) Relying on foreign aid
(b) Spending by borrowing from abroad
(c) Not spending enough to ensure development
(d) Spending in excess of revenue.

90. For growth saving rates have to be stepped up therefore planning strategy
(a) Should not bother about inequalities
(b) Should tolerate an accentuation of inequalities

(c) Should property reconcile the reduction of inequalities with the fast growth object
(d) None of these.

91. India's five year plan chiefly aimed at
(a) Fast growth rate, rapid reduction of inequalities and control of inflation
(b) Fast industrial growth, increased employment and better distribution
(c) Correcting disequlibrium in the economy caused by the war and the partition and initiating a process of all round balanced development
(d) Initiating a process of all round balanced development and fast growth agriculture.

92. On the eve of planning India's industrial structure however meagre in size was heavily titled towards the production of
(a) Consumer goods
(b) Defence production
(c) Light capital goods
(d) Heavy capital goods.

93. As a result of planned efforts:
(a) Dependence of the Indian economy on international economy has increased
(b) Dependence of the Indian economy on international economy has decreased
(c) Indian economy has achieved a greater degree of resistance to cope with disturbance in the international economy
(d) Indian economy has gone weak.

94. Self-reliance as an object of planning means
(a) Reduction in the dependence on foreign aid
(b) Diversification of domestic production for reduction in imports for certain critical commodities
(c) Promotion of exports to enable us to pay for imports from our own resource
(d) All of these.

95. The strategy of growth laid down in the draft plan—1978-83 emphasise the growth of
   (a) Heavy capital goods industries
   (b) Light capital goods industries
   (c) Consumer goods
   (d) Defence production.

96. The strategy underlying the second plan was the development of capital goods and basic industries. This was inherent in the Mahalanobis plan model which was based on the assumption that
   (a) It was essential for future rate of growth
   (b) Industry is to be developed faster than agriculture
   (c) Transformation of domestic goods into capital goods through trade was not possible
   (d) None of these.

97. In the seventh plan deficit financing was stated to raise
   (a) 4.5 per cent of total financial outlay
   (b) 7.2 per cent of total financial outlay
   (c) 1.7 per cent of total financial outlay
   (d) 2.3 per cent of total financial outlay.

98. There was a gap of three year between the termination of third year plan and the beginning of fourth plan which is generally called a plan holiday. This delay in the finalisation of the fourth plan was due to
   (a) Indo Pak conflict of 1965
   (b) Two successive year of drought
   (c) Sharp rise in prices and the consequent erosion of resources of the plan
   (d) All of the above.

99. About which five year plan the following statement is most appropriate. "It was never a five year plan. It was only a collection of annual development programmes, three of which precded its finalisation and the remaining two were not a part of it."
   (a) Third plan (b) Fourth plan
   (c) Fifth plan (d) Sixth plan.

100. In the first plan the share of public sector and private sector in the total sector and private sector in the total plan outlay was
   (a) 54.6 % and 45.4 % respectively
   (b) 46.4% and 53.6 % respectively
   (c) 60.3% and 39.7 % respectively
   (d) 52.9% and 47.1 % respectively.

101. India had a plan holiday
   (a) After the Sino-Indian war of 1962
   (b) After the drought of 1966
   (c) After the liberation of Bangladesh in 1971
   (d) During the Janta rule in 1977.

102. The overall aim of economic planning in India is
   (a) To increase industrial output
   (b) To increase national income
   (c) To generate rural employment
   (d) Growth with justice.

103. The concept of rolling plan was introduced in the
   (a) Third five year plan
   (b) Fourth five year plan
   (c) Fifth five year plan
   (d) Janata government draft of sixth five year plan.

104. The strategy of economic development adopted in our plan during period 1956-78 emphasised the growth of
   (a) Consumer goods industries
   (b) Defence production
   (c) Light capital goods industries
   (d) Heavy capital goods industries.

105. The 5 per cent annual growth rate income envisaged in the seventh plan refer to the growth rate of
   (a) Gross national product
   (b) Net national product
   (c) Gross domestic product

(d) Net domestic product.

106. Indian planning is based on the principles of domestic socialism. The essential features of domestic socialism are listed below. One of them is wrong. Which?

(a) It aims of reduction of enequalities of income and wealth
(b) It emphasises the growth of public sector to supplant the private sector
(c) It endeavours to check concentration of economic power and the growth of monopoly tendencies
(d) It aims at the provision of equal oppurtunities to all.

107. Self-reliance does not mean one of the following things. Which ?

(a) A long-term equilibrium in the balance of payment
(b) End of all imports
(c) Self-sufficiency in the capital goods sector
(d) Self-sufficiency in high technical man power.

108. Which one of the following is not a feature of India's economic planning

(a) Imperative planning
(b) Limited centralization
(c) Democratic socialism
(d) Indicative planning.

109. Which one of the following statements is not correct ?

(a) The Planning Commission of India is an advisory body
(b) The Planning Commission is set up by an act of Parliament
(c) The Planning Commission makes five year plan
(d) The Planning Commission implement five year plans.

110. Which one of the following has not been the state's objectives of our five year plans

(a) To reduce disparities in income distribution
(b) To achieve full employment

(c) To increase production
(d) To attain self reliance.

111. Which one of the following plans the orientation of economic policy to confirm the national goal of "social economy"?
(a) I st five year plan
(b) 2nd five year plan
(c) 5 th five year plan
(d) 3 rd five year plan.

112. Which one of the following was not a feature of the second plan?
(a) High production of foodgrain and commercial crops
(b) Inflationary trends
(c) Running down of foreign exchange reserves
(d) Suez crisis.

113. Which of the following is not an objective of India's economic planning ?
(a) Population growth
(b) Industrial growth
(c) Self reliance
(d) Employment generation.

114. Which of the following is true?
(a) Physical planning is more important than financial planning
(b) Financial planning is more important than physical planning
(c) Physical planning and financial planning are equally important
(d) Physical planning and financial planning are complementary.

115. The Draft fifth plan has to say that the basic objective of the community development programme is to "secure the fullest development of the material and human resources on an area basis and raise the rural community to higher level of living with active participation and on the initiative of the

(a) Increase in production and employment
(b) Application of the principle of self-reliance and co-operation on an extensive scale
(c) Harnessing rural manpower
(d) None of them.

116. Which of the following one is not a major achievement of Indian ecnomic planning
(a) Building a strong infrastructure
(b) Diversification of exports
(c) High growth rate of national income
(d) Development of science and technology.

ANSWERS

1.	(d)	2.	(d)	3.	(c)	4.	(b)
5.	(a)	6.	(c)	7.	(b)	8.	(c)
9.	(a)	10.	(b)	11.	(c)	12.	(c)
13.	(d)	14.	(d)	15.	(b)	16.	(c)
17.	(c)	18.	(b)	19.	(c)	20.	(b)
21.	(d)	22.	(c)	23.	(a)	24.	(c)
25.	(b)	26.	(a)	27.	(d)	28.	(c)
29.	(d)	30.	(c)	31.	(c)	32.	(a)
33.	(b)	34.	(d)	35.	(c)	36.	(a)
37.	(d)	38.	(a)	39.	(c)	40.	(b)
41.	(a)	42.	(d)	43.	(b)	44.	(c)
45.	(d)	46.	(c)	47.	(a)	48.	(b)
49.	(c)	50.	(a)	51.	(b)	52.	(a)
53.	(b)	54.	(b)	55.	(b)	56.	(c)
57.	(d)	58.	(c)	59.	(b)	60.	(d)
61.	(b)	62.	(b)	63.	(c)	64.	(a)
65.	(a)	66.	(d)	67.	(c)	68.	(b)
69.	(c)	70.	(c)	71.	(c)	72.	(b)
73.	(a)	74.	(c)	75.	(c)	76.	(b)
77.	(d)	78.	(c)	79.	(b)	80.	(c)
81.	(d)	82.	(a)	83.	(b)	84.	(d)
85.	(a)	86.	(b)	87.	(c)	88.	(c)
89.	(d)	90.	(c)	91.	(c)	92.	(a)

93.	(c)	94.	(d)	95.	(a)	96.	(c)
97.	(b)	98.	(d)	99.	(c)	100.	(b)
101.	(b)	102.	(d)	103.	(d)	104.	(d)
105.	(c)	106.	(b)	107.	(b)	108.	(a)
109.	(d)	110.	(b)	111.	(b)	112.	(a)
113.	(a)	114.	(d)	115.	(d)	116.	(a)

4
ECONOMIC GROWTH AND DEVELOPMENT

1. In any country where population grows roughly at a rate of 2% per annum for a stable per capita income the net national product must also record an annual increase of
   (a) 3% (b) 2%
   (c) 1.5% (d) 1%.
2. Infant industry argument for industrial protection was propounded by
   (a) Freidrich List (b) Raul Prebisch
   (c) Maurice jobb (d) Ranger Nurske.
3. Bulk of rural as well as urban unemployment in the LDC's is
   (a) Voluntary (b) Involuntary
   (c) Of shifting nature (d) None of the above.
4. Who says "a purely agricultural country is likely to be unprogressive even in agriculture"
   (a) Simon Kuznets (b) Harvey Leibenstein
   (c) J.K. Galbraith (d) None of the above.
5. According to the World Development Report 1991, income disparities are high in the
   (a) Less developed countries
   (b) Developed countries
   (c) Both (a) and (b)
   (d) None of the above.

6. The 'Balanced growth' theory was propounded by
   (a) H. Leibenstein (b) J. Viner
   (c) A.K. Sen (d) R. Nurkse.

7. Who has propounded the doctrine of Unbalanced growth?
   (a) R. Nurske
   (b) Rosentein Rodan
   (c) H. Myint
   (d) Albert O. Hirshman.

8. The demand for capital, in essence is a
   (a) Direct demand
   (b) Reciprocal demand
   (c) Derived demand
   (d) Complementary demand.

9. What are the obstacles to expand the market ?
   (a) Transport cost (b) Trade barriers
   (c) Exchange control (d) All of the above.

10. According to Nurske, the size of the capital depends on the
   (a) Level of income (b) Level of savings
   (c) Level of productivity (d) None of the above.

11. Capacity to buy means capacity to produce is analogous to
   (a) Say's law (b) Law of supply
   (c) Law of demand (d) Law of Keynes.

12. The techniques of production in underdeveloped countries are
   (a) Modern (b) Backward
   (c) Semi-modern (d) Ultra- modern.

13. Which techniques of production are preferable to India?
   (a) Labour-intensive techniques
   (b) Capital-intensive techniques
   (c) Both (a) and (b)
   (d) None of these.

14. The basic feature of an undeveloped country is
    (a) Low per capita income
    (b) Low productivity
    (c) High level of poverty
    (d) All the above.

15. Industrialization in the LDC's is
    (a) Enclave type
    (b) Capital intensive
    (c) Accommodative type
    (d) Labour intensive.

16. Before the Permanent Settlement of 1793 the Zamindars in India were the
    (a) Landlords
    (b) Actual tillers of the soil
    (c) Revenue farmers
    (d) Proprietors of the landlord assets.

17. Who wrote the book *"Poverty and Unbritish Rule in India"*
    (a) Romesh Chandra Dutta
    (b) P.C. Joshi
    (c) Surendra Nath Banerjee
    (d) Dada Bhai Naoroji.

18. Which of the following industry developed well before Independence?
    (a) Heavy Engineering (b) Machine tools
    (c) Chemical industries (d) Textiles.

19. The per capita income of India estimated in dollar terms in 1989 was merely
    (a) $ 320 (b) $ 330
    (c) $ 340 (d) $ 350.

20. The rate of capital accumulation before Independence was just
    (a) 5% of national income (b) 6% of national income
    (c) 7% of national incme (d) 8% of natonal income.

21. In 1950-51 the percentage share of GDP by agriculture and other primary activities accounted for
    (a) 56.4% (b) 45.5%
    (c) 39.5% (d) 33.9%.

22. In percentage terms the share of agriculture and primary activities in India's GDP over the planning period has
    (a) Declined a little (b) Substaintially declined
    (c) Increased (d) Increased moderately.

23. Of the total production in the manufacturing sector in 1950-51 small scale sector accounted for about
    (a) 30% (b) 40%
    (c) 50% (d) 60%.

24. In the agricultural sector the output has increased at the rate of -------- % per annum over the plan period.
    (a) 2% (b) 2.2%
    (c) 3% (d) 3.5%.

25. Industry recorded a trend growth rates of
    (a) 5% per annum (b) 5.4 % per annum
    (c) 6% per annum (d) 6.4 % per annum.

26. Per annum trend growth rates of services sector is around
    (a) 5% (b) 6%
    (c) 7% (d) 8%.

27. In the early 1950's the share of agriculture in the GDP in India was more than 50%. Now it has come down to about
    (a) 30% (b) 30%
    (c) 32% (d) 33%.

28. During the planning period industrial sector has undergone a
    (a) Structural change
    (b) Cyclical change
    (c) Contra- cyclical change
    (d) Industrial change.

29. The growing shares of the services sector in the GDP reflect the expansion of
    (a) Agriculture in the country
    (b) Foreign trade
    (c) Economic infrastructure
    (d) Public sector in the economy.

30. The tertiary sector accounts for about .... of the labour force
    (a) 1/3 rd (b) 1/4 th
    (c) 1/5 th (d) 1/6 th.

31. "Socialist pattern of society" was envisaged in the
    (a) First plan (b) Second plan
    (c) Third plan (d) Fourth plan.

32. The share of Public Administration and Defence in the GDP is
    (a) Steady rising (b) Falling proportionately
    (c) Remaining unchanged (d) Uncountable.

33. Over the period spanning from 1951 to 1981 industrial sectors share of absorbing labour force has increased by:
    (a) 5% (b) 4%
    (c) 3% (d) 2%.

34. The ratio of labour to both land and capital in Agriculture showed a tendency to
    (a) Rise (b) Fall
    (c) Remain constant (d) None of the above.

35. The marginal productivity of labour in Agriculture in India has turned out to be
    (a) Positive (b) Negative
    (c) Zero (d) Infinity.

36. To raise output per man hour requires raising the ratio of
    (a) Capital of labour
    (b) Capital of output
    (c) Labour to capital
    (d) Labour to total factors availability.

37. Even before the Independence India had a fairly important public sector the most important components of which was the
    (a) Ship building industry
    (b) Defence
    (c) Railway system
    (d) Cement industry.

38. In respect of iron ore and coal reserve India ranks in the world
    (a) First (b) Second
    (c) Third (d) Fifth.

39. The disguised unemployment in rural sector has tended to become widespread in recent years because the technical progress has become more and more
    (a) Capital intensive (b) Labour intensive
    (c) Important intensive (d) Both (a) and (b).

40. State capitalism basically implies
    (a) A socialistic economy
    (b) A capitalist economy
    (c) A mixed economy
    (d) None of the above.

41. The share of the public sector in the national output in India is
    (a) More than 50%
    (b) More than 30 % but less 50%
    (c) Less than 25%
    (d) 27%.

42. Some economists taking rate of the public sector and economic planning in India's economy prefer to characterise it is
    (a) State monopoly
    (b) State induced socialism
    (c) State induced privatisation
    (d) State capitalism.

43. Over the time span of the decades since the inception of planning the big buiseness have been able to increase their assets by

(a) Thrice (b) 5 times
(c) 7 times (d) More than 10 times.

44. The investment made in the state sector during the past four decades were arround

(a) 60 % (b) 55%
(c) 45% (d) 40%.

45. Indian planning as more related to

(a) Socialism (b) Egalitarian society
(c) Capitalism (d) None of these.

46. In India the mixed economy framework has tended to favour

(a) Relatively rich (b) Relatively poor
(c) Poorest of the poor (d) All sections of society.

47. India still remains one of the most underdeveloped nations in terms of

(a) Natural resources
(b) The avaibility of capital
(c) Per capita income
(d) Per capita expenditure.

48. India has per capita income higher than

(a) Italy (b) Pakistan
(c) Cuba (d) Zaire.

49. In 1989, agriculture contributed .... % of the G.D.P

(a) 30 % (b) 35 %
(c) 39 % (d) 40 %.

50. In 1950-51, the net saving investment rate in this country was around

(a) 7 % (b) 8 %
(c) 9 % (d) 10 %.

51. Over the planning period both saving and investment rates have
(a) Fallen (b) Risen
(c) Remained constant (d) Entrepreneures.

52. In the theory of economic growth to seph A Schumeter has assigned vital role to
(a) Agriculture (b) Commerce
(c) Industry (d) Entrepreneures.

53. Over a period of about four decades, the trend rate of growth of national income was around
(a) 7.5 % (b) 6.3 %
(c) 5 % (d) 3.8 %.

54. The target in the first plan had fixed a .... per cent rise in NNP, but the achievement was .... per cent
(a) 10,9 (b) 11,18
(c) 18,11 (d) 12,14.

55. The target in the second plan was to raise NNP by .... per cent but the actual rise in NNP was .... per cent
(a) 25, 21.4 (b) 26, 20.1
(c) 25, 22.5 (d) 27, 25.

56. The third plan contemplated a ....per cent increase in NNP but is rose merely by .... per cent
(a) 28, 9.5 (b) 29, 10.6
(c) 30, 11.7 (d) 31, 12.1.

57. During the seventh plan the rate of increase in NNP has been around
(a) 6 per cent (b) 5.5 per cent
(c) 5 per cent (d) 4.6 per cent.

58. During the third plan, the per capita income
(a) Registered a spectacular growth
(b) Remainded almost static
(c) Had actually declined
(d) Had become Zero.

59. The planning experience in India tells us that planning in India had remained

(a) Inadequate (b) Adequate
(c) Dynamic one (d) A static one.

60. Over the four decades, starting from 1950-51 India's per capita income in 1980-81 prices has increased by around

(a) 60% (b) 70%
(c) 80% (d) 90%.

61. According to the Monopolies Enquiry Commission in 1963-64 there were

(a) 90 big business houses in India
(b) 80 big business houses in India
(c) 75 big business houses in India
(d) 65 big business houses in India.

62. The Monopoly Enquiry Commission estimated that of the non government and non-banking companies in India the big buiseness controlled

(a) 44 % of the paid up capital
(b) 50% of the paid up capital
(c) 54 % of the paid up capital
(d) 59 % of the paid up capital.

63. Over the years per head agriculture and land steadily declined in this country was around

(a) Low land reclamation
(b) Rapid growth industry
(c) Rapid growth population
(d) None of the above.

64. Occupational distribution of population in India during the planning period

(a) Changed significantly
(b) Remained almost changed
(c) Marked a progressive note
(d) Market a retardation.

65. An absolute pre-condition for economic growth in poor country is
    (a) A fall in the birth rate
    (b) Capital formation
    (c) Substaned low interest rates
    (d) The creation of banking system.

66. The classical theory of economic development failed to take in to account
    (a) The rate of the state
    (b) Technical innovation
    (c) Distribution of income
    (d) None of the above.

67. Inequalities of incomes are marked in underdeveloped countries in
    (a) Agricultural sector (b) Manufacturing sector
    (c) Service sector (d) All of these.

68. For economic development Schumpeter gives importance to
    (a) Creditors (b) Entrepreneures
    (c) Innovation (d) Invention.

69. Which of the following is a necessary condition for the high rate of modern economic growth ?
    (a) Continuous technological progress
    (b) Development of urban centre
    (c) High rate of population growth
    (d) Expansion of money supply in to the economy.

70. To achieve creditable per capita growth rates of the economy the proportion of the GDP that must be saved is
    (a) 2-3 % (b) 5-6 %
    (c) 8-10 % (d) 12-15%.

71. Which of the following is an example of economic overhead ?
    (a) Schools (b) Sanitary facilities
    (c) Hospitals (d) Roads and Railways.

72. India's natural resources are
(a) Rich
(b) Poor
(c) Small as compound to the size of the country
(d) None of the above.

73. Throughout the post-Independence period agriculture has provided work to
(a) 2/3 rd or more of the labour force
(b) 1/3 rd or less of the labour force
(c) 1/2 of the labour force
(d) 1/4 of the labour force.

74. Which of the following is not included in the teritory sector?
(a) Transport communication and trade
(b) Banking and insurance
(c) Public administration, defence and other services
(d) Construction and manufacturing.

75. The amount of investment and its form is great determined by
(a) Government incentives
(b) The price of the industrial products
(c) The interest rate that prevail in the money market
(d) All of these.

76. The Industries (Development and Regulation) Act, 1951 was passed to provide
(a) Development assistance to the industries
(b) A regulation system for industries
(c) Oppurtunity for setting up of new industrial units
(d) None of these.

77. According to the Monopolies Enquiry Commission in 1963-64 there were
(a) 90 big business houses in India
(b) 80 big business house in India
(c) 75 big business buiseness house in India
(d) 65 big business house in India.

78. The public sector in India has been set up to
    (a) Give a big push to the economy
    (b) Overcome the 'low level equilibrium trap of the development
    (c) To develop the strategic sectors of the economy
    (d) Promote all the above.

79. The proportion of working population in agriculture during the first two decades of planning had
    (a) Declined rapidly
    (b) Increased substantially
    (c) Vertically remained static
    (d) Shifted to the urban industrialized sector.

80. Occupation distribution of popualtion in India during the planning period
    (a) Changed significantly
    (b) Remained almost unchanged
    (c) Marked a progressive note
    (d) Marked a retardation.

81. It is asserted that the pattern of growth in under-developed countries is a dualistic. One the term dualism refer to
    (a) Two way approach to economic growth
    (b) Co-existence of developed and under-developed sectors
    (c) Co-existence of consumption and production sector
    (d) Co-existence of capital intensive as well as capital light industries.

82. The U.N experts (1951) have defined an underdeveloped country as the one in which per capita real income is low when compared with the per capita real income of
    (a) U.S.A, Canada, Australia and western Europe
    (b) U.S.A., Japan, U.A.E., England
    (c) U.S.A, Japan, West Germany and France
    (d) U.S.A, Japan, Canada, Australia.

83. The rate of capital formation in underdeveloped economy is low due to
   (a) Widespread poverty
   (b) Demonstration effect to follow suit the consumption pattern of the developed countries
   (c) Lack of natural resources
   (d) High defence expenditure.

84. Kuznets a noted economist, assets that the income disparities in the developed countries are low because of
   (a) Greater reliance on indirect tax to mop up resource for the benefit of the society
   (b) Progressive of direct taxes and free economic assistance to the lower income strata
   (c) Trickle down' effect
   (d) Adopting a programme of building the minimum needs of the poor.

85. Underdeveloped countries are essentially agrarian in their character .... it means
   (a) About 70 % to 90% of the population depends on agriculture in these countries
   (b) Major part of the national income originates in the agriculture sector
   (c) Share of agriculture is less than share of employment in agriculture
   (d) All of these.

86. According to 'Unbalanced growth' theory unequal development of various sector causes income inequality
   (a) Unequal development of various sector causes income inequality
   (b) Unequal development conditions for rapid development
   (c) Unequal development of various sector leads to technological dualism
   (d) Unequal balance of different sector create disproportions in the economy.

87. According to the "vicious circle of poverty doctrine" poverty is widespread in the LDC because of
(a) Low income low savings of the people
(b) Low capital formation
(c) Low productivity
(d) The combined effect of (a), (b), (c).

88. Low aborption capacity on the industrial labour force point out that the expansion of the industrial sector
(a) Has failed to transform the structure of the economy
(b) Has helped to change the agrarian structure
(c) Basically concentrated in the Hi-tech area
(d) Significance nothing of the above.

89. In India the employment opportunities have failed to grow rapidly because
(a) Fixed technical co-efficiency in industrial sector
(b) Low complementary of industrial structure
(c) Variable technical co-efficients
(d) Limited availability of raw materials.

90. Economic development can be defined simply as
(a) National Income keeping up with population increases
(b) An increase in real per capita income over an extended period of time
(c) An increase in national income from one year to another
(d) Increase in real investment over many years.

91. Economic development can be measured with the help of
(a) Increase in GDP
(b) Increase in NNP
(c) Increase in per capita income at current price
(d) Increase in per capita income at constant price.

92. The difference between 'Development' and 'Growth' is that
(a) The former generally refers to underdeveloped countries whereas the latter generally refers to developed countries

(b) The former generally refers to fundamental changes in structure of the economy' social attitudes etc. whereas the latter generally refers to a stedy change in an already well established economy
(c) Both (a) and (b)
(d) Neither (a) and (b).

93. Agriculture has an important role to play in the development process because
(a) A balanced approach to growth is necessary
(b) The vast majority of an undeveloped country resources are engaged in agriculture
(c) Underdeveloped countries do better in agriculture
(d) None of these.

94. The growth of the low income countries depends on
(a) Social and economic condition in them only
(b) International conditions only
(c) International and internal condition though more on the latter
(d) International and internal condition though more on the former.

95. Economic growth can be measured in terms of changes in
(a) Gross domestic product per head of the occupied population per annum
(b) Real national income per head of the total population per annum
(c) Gross national product per head of the working population per annum
(d) Average cost of living of working class families.

96. In the underdeveloped countries, death rate has sharply declined due to
(a) Increase of the per capita income
(b) Increase in the level of education
(c) Improvement in the medical facilities
(d) Increase in the people's concern for their life.

97. Which of the following is a necessary condition for the high rate of modern economic growth?
   (a) Continuous technological progress
   (b) Development of urban centres
   (c) High rate of population growth
   (d) Expansion of money supply into the economy.

98. Economic growth in underdeveloped economies is accompained by
   (a) High rate of growth of population and small change in occupational structure
   (b) Increased rate of capital formation and decreasing deth rate
   (c) Sustained rise in product per capita and high population gowth rate
   (d) All of the above.

99. Term 'real' is specified in the definition of economic development because
   (a) GNP statistics are affected by changes in price level
   (b) GNP statistics are estimated each year in current rupee terms
   (c) Real GNP is a figure corrected for price changes and isolates Growth in real or physical terms from the increases in price.
   (d) None of these.

100. Normally speaking revolutions in agriculture
   (a) Must pecede industrial revolution
   (b) Must accompany industrial revolution
   (c) Must succeed industrial revolution
   (d) Must take place after a lag.

101. Modern economic growth has been charcterised by
   (a) High rate of growth of population but no change in occupational structure
   (b) Increased rate of capital formation but no change in per capita product
   (c) High growth rate of population and a sustained rise in per capita product

(d) High growth rate of population with continuous rise in birth rate.

102. As an index of net contribution of goods and services, NNP is better than GNP. Why is it that even than it is not universally accepted as a measure of economic growth?

(a) Because it is not easily calculated
(b) Because it is vague
(c) Because underdeveloped countries cannot know it
(d) Because it is arrived after deducting depreciation, the estimate of which both difficult and arbitrary.

103. Capital accumulation

(a) Facilitates capital widening
(b) Makes capital deepening possible
(c) Encourages introduction of new technology
(d) Affects the proficiency of labour.

104. Capital output ratio refers to

(a) Units of capital required to produce consumer goods
(b) Unit of capital requirqd to produce one unit of output
(c) Amount of capital required to instal a capital asset
(d) None of these.

105. Kuznets' preference for real GNP over real per capita GNP as a measure of economic growth arises from

(a) The desirability to concentrate on growth of output alone
(b) The need to combine output growth and population growth
(c) The desirability to concentrate on the factors speeding economic growth and to analyse the population problem separately
(d) All of these.

106. A rise in per capita product usually means

(a) An even greater increase in product per capita of labour input
(b) Decrease in product per unit of labour input

(c) Proportionate increase in product per unit of labour input

(d) Proportionate decrease in product per unit of labour unit.

107. Besides poverty, developing economy have many other common characteristics, like

(a) Percentage of their population engaged in agriculture is generally very high

(b) Technological dualism prevails in all these countries

(c) The capital -labour ratio is low

(d) All of the above.

108. Saving is

(a) The major determinant of growth

(b) The only determinant of growth

(c) One of the determinants of growth

(d) Not concerned with growth.

109. In poor countries

(a) Only the supply of capital is low

(b) Only the demand for capital is low

(c) Both the supply of and demand for capital are low

(d) None of them is true.

110. Ricardo predicted the economy can/would end in a stationary state because

(a) People would tire of working

(b) The economy would run out of gold

(c) Innovation would dry up

(d) The economy would run out of arable land.

111. The occupational distribution of labour is

(a) The same in developed and underdeveloped countries

(b) Different in developed and underdeveloped countries

(c) Only a shade different in developed and underdeveloped countries

(d) Nothing can be said.

112. One of the possible sources of untapped private domestic saving in less developed countries as state by economists is
   (a) There can be voluntary reduction in consumption there by freeing additional resources for investment
   (b) Unemployed or underemployed labour can be absorbed in the productive economy, increase national income and the possibility of saving
   (c) The government can require citizen to purchase long term, non-negotiable bonds, and finance national investment programmes through private savings
   (d) Establishment of a state marketing board for exports may enable the government to purchase domestic goods.

113. Which of the following statements is correct? Economic growth is associated with
   (a) A decline in the share of the agricultural sector both in labour force and income
   (b) With a rise in the share of the manufacturing sector, more conspicuous in income than in the labour force
   (c) With a rise in the share of the service sector in the labour force, but not necessarily a rise in national product
   (d) All the above.

114. Which of the following is an incorrect statement ?
   (a) A scientific discovery can be major or minor
   (b) A scientific discovery is an addition to knowledge
   (c) An invention is a minor knowledge applied to day to day knowledge of production
   (d) An invention is a vested combination of already existing knowledge to a useful end.

115. Which of the following is not necessarily true?
   (a) Proportional tax is progressive
   (b) An increased rate of tax will increase government revenue
   (c) Direct tax can be related to ability to pay
   (d) A subsidy is a negative tax.

116. Which of the following is false? ICORS are rough estimates because
   (a) No one can really tell how much capital is needed for an investment project
   (b) ICORS are measured in gross net
   (c) ICORS are normally measured over extended periods of time
   (d) ICORS ignore many important factors contributing to growth.

117. Which of the following statements is not correct in the context of modern economic growth ?
   (a) It is in substance an application of the industrial system based on
   (b) It calls for the capacity of society to absorb changes and adopt innovation
   (c) It means not only growth of output but changes of social structure also
   (d) It means an expansion of production without change in techniques and productivity.

118. Which of the following is not fully correct?
   (a) Science is the basis of modern technology. Modern technology is the base of modern economic growth.
   (b) Modern technology is the base of modern economic growth
   (c) Attitudes of people change and economic growth follows
   (d) Growth is a time determined process.

119. Which of the following is correct with relation to Kahn
   (a) Importance of exports for a developing country
   (b) An estimate of difference between private and social costs
   (c) The input-output analysis
   (d) All of the above.

120. Which of the following is not a correct statement about Higgin's technological dualism theory ?

(a) It presents an historical evolution of the modern and traditional sectors leading to a steady rise in unemployment in the latter sector
(b) It is superior to Boek's social dualism theory
(c) It assumes the existence of the same production function in the two sectors
(d) Production in the modern sector is invariably carried on with fixed technological coefficient.

121. Which one of the following is correct?
(a) India adopted planning as her way of life because she wanted to quicken industrialisation and economic development with optimum utilization of resources and reduction of enequalities : False
(b) The first plan was a success because there was no plan at all and nature was very favourable : True
(c) The second plan was not only an ambitious plan but also an unfortunate plan because it failed on all fronts due to many constraints : False
(d) The Third Plan in general presented a grim picture of the state of the Indian economy and also underlined the total failure of planning efforts: True.

122. Which one of the following is not necessarily true ?
(a) A proportional tax is progressive
(b) An increased rate of tax will increase government revenue
(c) Direct tax can be related to ability to pay
(d) A subsidy is a negative tax.

123. Which one of the following is not true regarding Feldman's model of economic growth ?
(a) It integrates the elements of growth process with the Marxian scheme of reproduction
(b) The economy consist of two sectors the consumer goods sector and the capital goods sector
(c) There is no intermediate goods production
(d) The average propensity to save determines the rate of growth of income.

124. Which of the following statements is correct ?
   (a) In an advanced country during depression the industries, machines, managers and workers as well as the consumption habits all are present but in underdeveloped countries this is not so
   (b) The remedies applied in advanced economies to rectify imbalances between demand and supply are not properly applicable to backward economics
   (c) Both (a) and (b) are correct
   (d) Neither (a) nor (b) is correct.

125. Which of the following is not the characteristic of a mixed economy
   (a) Private ownership of the means of the production
   (b) Co-existence of private and public sector
   (c) Decisive role of the government about the priority of the production decision
   (d) The predominance of the market mechanism.

126. Match the following:

i. Japan	(A) Low density and moderate growth
ii. Australia	(B) Underdeveloped and thickly populated
iii. Brazil	(C) High density and rapid growth
iv. East Asia	(D) Developed and low density.

   (a) I.A, ii. B, iii.C, iv. D
   (b) I.B, ii.C, iii.A, iv. B
   (c i.C, ii.D, iii.A, ivB,
   (d) I.C, ii.A, iii.B, iv.D.

127. Match the following:

i.	Vicious circle of poverty	A. H. Leifenstein
ii.	Critical minimum effort thesis	B. W.W Rostow
iii.	Stages of economic growth	C. Rosente Inpandan
iv.	Unbalanced growth	D. R. Nurske

   (a) I.B, ii.C, iii. D, iv. A
   (b) I.C, ii.D, iii.A, iv.B
   (c) I.D, ii.A, iii.B, iv.C
   (d) I.A, ii.B, iii.C, iv.D.

128. Country rate of growth is determined directly to the
   1. Proportion of income invested
   2. Size of the multiplier
   3. Productivity of its capital

   (a) II and III (b) I and III
   (c) I and II (d) III only.

129. If a country dependent population increased while its occupied population remained the same it could experience
   1, Positive economic progress with negative growth
   2. Negative progress with positive growth
   3. positive progress with positive growth
   4. Negative progress with negative growth

   (a) 1, 3, 4, only (b) 2 and 4 only
   (c) None of them (d) All of them.

130. Economic progress causes unemployment because of the
   1. Higher rates of saving
   2. Immovability of labour
   3. Deficiency of aggregate monetary demand

   (a) 1 and 3 (b) 1 and 2
   (c) 2 only (d) All of them.

131. An increase in the propensity of saving and in capital per head of the working population will sustain a higher growth rate if supplemented by an improvement in
   1. The quality of the labour force
   2. The quality of work method
   3. The efficiency of work method
   4. The design and efficiency of capital goods

   (a) 2 only (b) 1 and 2 only
   (c) 2 and 3 only (d) All of them.

132. Harrod defines natural rate of growth as the rate
   1. At which the natural resources available to the economy are utilised
   2. Of advance which the increase of population and technological improvement allow

3. of advance which of the availability natural resource allow
4. Which is also called full-employment rate of growth

(a) 1 only (b) 1, 2 and 3
(c) 2, 3 and 4 only (d) 1, 2, 4 only.

133. Comparison of the growth rate of different countries have to be used with care because
1. The relevant statistics vary considerably in adequacy and reliability
2. Goods vary considerably in their importance in different countries
3. There is no precise way of linking prices stated in different currencies
4. The extent to which commodities have prices attached to them varies with different economic structure

(a) 1, 2, 4 only (b) 2, 4 only
(c) 1, 2, 4 only (d) All of them.

ANSWERS

1.	(b)	2.	(a)	3.	(b)	4.	(c)
5.	(a)	6.	(d)	7.	(d)	8.	(c)
9.	(d)	10.	(c)	11.	(a)	12.	(b)
13.	(a)	14.	(d)	15.	(a)	16.	(c)
17.	(d)	18.	(d)	19.	(c)	20.	(a)
21.	(a)	22.	(b)	23.	(d)	24.	(b)
25.	(b)	26.	(a)	27.	(d)	28.	(a)
29.	(c)	30.	(a)	31.	(b)	32.	(a)
33.	(c)	34.	(a)	35.	(c)	36.	(a)
37.	(c)	38.	(c)	39.	(d)	40.	(c)
41.	(c)	42.	(d)	43.	(d)	44.	(c)
45.	(c)	46.	(a)	47.	(c)	48.	(d)
49.	(a)	50.	(a)	51.	(b)	52.	(d)
53.	(d)	54.	(b)	55.	(a)	56.	(c)
57.	(b)	58.	(b)	59.	(a)	60.	(d)
61.	(c)	62.	(a)	63.	(c)	64.	(b)
65.	(b)	66.	(b)	67.	(d)	68.	(c)
69.	(a)	70.	(d)	71.	(d)	72.	(a)

73.	(a)	74.	(d)	75.	(c)	76.	(b)
77.	(c)	78.	(a)	79.	(c)	80.	(b)
81.	(b)	82.	(a)	83.	(a)	84.	(b)
85.	(d)	86.	(b)	87.	(d)	88.	(a)
89.	(a)	90.	(b)	91.	(d)	92.	(c)
93.	(b)	94.	(c)	95.	(b)	96.	(c)
97.	(a)	98.	(d)	99.	(c)	100.	(a)
101.	(c)	102.	(d)	103.	(c)	104.	(b)
105.	(c)	106.	(a)	107.	(d)	108.	(c)
109.	(c)	110.	(d)	111.	(b)	112.	(b)
113.	(d)	114.	(c)	115.	(b)	116.	(c)
117.	(d)	118.	(d)	119.	(b)	120	(c)
121.	(b)	122.	(d)	123.	(c)	124.	(c)
125.	(c)	126.	(c)	127.	(c)	128.	(b)
129.	(a)	130.	(c)	131.	(d)	132.	(c)
133.	(d)						

5
THE LAW OF DEMAND AND ELASTICITY

1. The law of demand refers to
   (a) Price-supply relationship
   (b) Price-cost relationship
   (c) Price-demand relationship
   (d) Price-income relationship.

2. In a typical demand schedule quantity demanded
   (a) Varies directly with price
   (b) Varies proportionally with price
   (c) Varies inversely with price
   (d) Is independent of price.

3. An exceptional demand curve is one that stops
   (a) Upwards to the right (b) Downward to the right
   (c) Upwards ot the left (d) Horizontally.

4. Two goods have to be consumed simultaneously are
   (a) Identical (b) Complementary
   (c) Substitutes (d) None of these.

5. Which of the following pairs of commodities is an example of substitutes
   (a) Coffee and milk
   (b) Diamond and cow
   (c) Pen and ink
   (d) Mustard oil and coconut oil.

6. Bread and butter lamb and mint sauce illustrate the type of inter-related demand known as
   (a) Rival demand
   (b) Composite demand
   (c) Competitive demand
   (d) Joint demand.

7. When an individual's income falls (while every things else remain the same) his demand for inferior goods
   (a) Increases
   (b) Decreases
   (c) Remain uncharged
   (d) We cannot without additional information.

8. An income demand curve for inferior commodity always slopes
   (a) Upward to the right
   (b) Backwards
   (c) Downward to the right
   (d) Horizontally.

9. When the price of the substitute of commodity x falls Re demand for x
   (a) Rises (b) Falls
   (c) Remains unchanged (d) Any of above.

10. When the both the prices of a substitute and the price of a complement of commodity x rise the demand for x
   (a) Rises
   (b) Falls
   (c) Remains unchanged
   (d) All of the above.

11. A demand curve regressive at the lower end depicts the case of
   (a) A normal good
   (b) A good commonly demand
   (c) An inferior good
   (d) A good demanded urgents.

12. When the demand curve is a rectangular hyperbola it represents
    (a) Unitary elastic demand
    (b) Perfectly elastic demand
    (c) Perfectly inelastic demand
    (d) Relatively elastic demand.

13. If the percentage increase in the quantity of a commodity demanded is smaller than the percentage fall in its prices elasticity of demand is
    (a) > 1 (b) = 1
    (c) < 1 (d) Zero.

14. If total consumer expenditure on a goods falls as its price falls this indicate that
    (a) E<1
    (b) Inferior goods
    (c) Taste for it is declining
    (d) It is being produced under condition of decreasing cost.

15. A negative income elasticity of demand for a commodity indicates that as income falls the amount of the commodity purchased
    (a) Rises (b) Falls
    (c) Remain unchanged (d) Any of the above.

16. Consider a demand curve which takes the form of a straight line cutting both axis. Elasticity at the mid point of the line would be
    (a) 0 (b) 1.0
    (c) 1.5 (d) 2.0.

17. When with a change in price the total outlay on a commodity remains constant it is a case of
    (a) Perfect elasticity
    (b) Perfect inelasticity
    (c) Unit elasticity
    (d) Zero elasticity.

18. Cross elasticity of demand between perfect and automobiles is

(a) Negative (b) Zero
(c) Hight (d) Infinite.

19. A straight line downward sloping demand curve implies that as price fall the elasticity of demand

(a) Increase (b) Decrease
(c) Remains the same (d) Is zero.

20. In the longer period permitting adjustment demand is likely to be

(a) Inelastic (b) Elastic
(c) Unit elastic (d) Cannot be known.

21. Elasticity of demand is equal to unity while marginal revenue is

(a) Positive (b) Zero
(c) Negative (d) Indeterminate.

22. A demand curve which takes the form of a horizontal line parallel to the quanity axis illustrates elasticity which is

(a) Zero (b) Infinite
(c) > 1 (d) < 1.

23. If the percentage increase in the quantity of a commodity demanded is smaller than the percentage fall in its price the coefficient of price elasticity of demand is

(a) Greater than 1 (b) Equal to 1
(c) Less than 1 (d) Zero.

24. If the quantity of a commodity demanded remain unchanged as its price changes the coefficient of price elasticity of demand is

(a) Greater than 1 (b) Equal to 1
(c) Less than 1 (d) Zero.

25. Which of the following commodities has the lowest elasticity of demand ?

(a) Milk (b) Black pepper
(c) Eggs (d) Car.

26. When the income elasticity of demand is greater than unity the commodity is
    (a) Necessity (b) A luxary
    (c) An inferior goods (d) A non-related good.

27. At low prices demand is likely to be
    (a) More elastic
    (b) Less elastic
    (c) Unit elastic
    (d) Cannot be known.

28. Ceteris paribus a change in the price of a commodity causes the quantity purchased of its complements to move
    (a) In the same direction
    (b) In the opposite direction
    (c) In an insignificant manner
    (d) Cannot be known.

29. If a result of an increase in price total outlay on a commodity decreases its price elasticity of demand is
    (a) Perfectly elastic
    (b) Relatively elastic
    (c) Unit elastic
    (d) Relatively inelastic.

30. In case of an inferior commodity the income elasticity of demand is
    (a) Positive (b) Unitary
    (c) Negative (d) Infinity.

31. Suppose your income increases by 10% and demand for commodity increases by 10% then the income elasticity of demand is
    (a) Negative (b) Positive
    (c) Zero (d) Infinity.

32. In the case of a superior commodity the income elasticity of demand is
    (a) Positive (b) Zero
    (c) Negative (d) Infinity.

33. A negative income elasticity of demand for a commodity indicates that as income falls the amount of the commodity purchased

(a) Remain unchanged (b) Falls
(c) Rises (d) None of these.

34. At a point above the middle of the straight line demand curve elasticity of demand is

(a) Less than one (b) Equal to one
(c) More than one (d) None of these.

35. Elasticity of supply for a positively sloped straight line supply curve that intersect the price axis is

(a) Zero (b) =1
(c) >1 (d) Constant.

36. Assuming that the price of Kerosene stove and gas stove falls within the same range. The cross elasticity of demand between them would be

(a) Very low (b) High
(c) Infinite (d) Low.

37. Two commodities are considered to be perfect substitutes for each other if the elasticity of substitution is

(a) Positive (b) Negative
(c) Zero (d) Infinite.

38. A commodity having a number of uses will face a demand which is

(a) Unit elasticity (b) Inelastic
(c) Elastic (d) None of these.

39. A fall in the price of a commodity whose demand curve is a rectangular hyperbola causes total expenditure in the commodity to

(a) Increase
(b) Decrease
(c) Remain unchanged
(d) None of these.

40. The Horizontal demand curve for a commodity shows that its demand is
    (a) Highly elastic (b) Perfectly inelastic
    (c) Perfectly elastic (d) Moderately elastic.

41. Of the following commodities which has the lowest elasticity of demand
    (a) Car (b) Salt
    (c) Tea (d) Houses.

42. With an increase in income a consumer is expected to buy more of
    (a) An inferior goods (b) A Giffen goods
    (c) A normal goods (d) All kinds of goods.

43. A situation where the amount spent by consumers in a commodities is constant when price changes is known as
    (a) Equilibrium (b) Perfect elasticity
    (c) Unitary elasticity (d) Backward sloping.

44. Elasticity (E) expressed by the formula $1>E>0$ is
    (a) Perfect elasticity (b) Relative elastic
    (c) Unitary elastic (d) Relative inelastic.

45. A necessity with substitutes will have
    (a) Inelasticity of demand
    (b) Elasticity of demand
    (c) More elasticity of demand
    (d) None of these.

46. An inferior commodity is one whose quantity demand decreases when income of the consumer
    (a) Decreases (b) Increases
    (c) Remains constant (d) None of the above.

47. In case the two commodities are good substitutes cross elasticity will be
    (a) Positive (b) Unitary
    (c) Negative (d) Infinite.

48. In case the two commodities are complements cross elasticity will be
    (a) Positive (b) Unitary
    (c) Negative (d) Infinite.

49. An increase in the price of a commodity when demand is inelastic causes the total expenditure of consumers of the commodity to
    (a) Increase
    (b) Decrease
    (c) Remain unchanged
    (d) Any of the above.

50. Demand for electricity is
    (a) Inelastic (b) Elastic
    (c) Less elastic (d) None of these.

51. At high prices, demand is likely to be
    (a) More elastic (b) Less elastic
    (c) Unit elastic (d) Cannot be known.

52. The verticle demand curve for commodity shows that its demand is
    (a) Highly elastic
    (b) Perfectly inelastic
    (c) Fairly elastic
    (d) Moderate elastic.

53. The coefficient of price elasticity of demand between two points is called
    (a) Income elasticity (b) Arc elasticity
    (c) Cross easticity (d) None of the above.

54. Cross elasticity of demand for petrol is the responsiveness of demand for petrol to a change in
    (a) Price of car (b) Price of petrol
    (c) Change of income (d) None of the above.

55. In economics demand means
    (a) Desire of the society to purchase all that is on the

market at a given period of time

(b) The desire and willingness of the individual for all the goods and services for his standard of living

(c) At a given price per unit of time the desirability and willingness of an individual to purchase goods and services

(d) The willingness of the individual for all the goods and services for his necessaries.

56. The demand function for a commodity is defined as

(a) Price of complementary goods as a function of the goods own price

(b) Quantity demanded as a function of the price of other goods

(c) Quality demanded as a function of the goods own price the price of substitutes and the buyers income

(d) Quantity demanded as function of its own price holding the price of other goods and the buyers income fixed.

57. The law of demand

(a) Upward shift of the demand curve is there fore not useful

(b) Cannot be varified and is therefore unrealistic

(c) Is of fundamental importance in economics and lead to bread conclusions

(d) Can be completely discarded.

58. Normally when price per unit of a good falls its

(a) Quantity demanded increases

(b) Quantity demanded remains constant

(c) None of these happens

(d) Market demand for any good is a function of the.

59. Price over unit of the good

(a) Price per unit of other goods

(b) Income of consumers

(c) Tastes of consumers

(d) All of the above.

60. The demand curve for a commodity is generally drawn on the assumption that
    (a) The commodity has no substitutes
    (b) Tastes income and all other prices remain constant
    (c) The average house hold consists of two persons
    (d) Purchases of the commodity are made by a free market.

61. When the law of demands operate the demand curve
    (a) Slopes downward from left to right
    (b) Slopes upward from left to right
    (c) Slopes upward from right to left
    (d) Parallel to horozontal axis.

62. A typical demand curve cannot be
    (a) Convex to the origin
    (b) A straight line parallel to y-axis
    (c) A straight line parallel to x-axis
    (d) Raising upwards to the right.

63. Ceteris paribus clause in law of demand does not mean
    (a) The price of the commodity does not change
    (b) The price of its substitutes does not change
    (c) The income of the consumer does not change
    (d) The price of complementary goods does not change.

64. A commodity the price of which has fallen but is expected to fall further will present a demand curve
    (a) Regressive of the lower end
    (b) Regressive at the upper end
    (c) Linked in the middle
    (d) Downward sloping to right.

65. An income-demand curve for a "luxury commodity" slopes
    (a) Upwards to the right from the origin
    (b) Vertically
    (c) Upwards from left to right only beyond a certain level of consumers income
    (d) Horizontally

66. "Change in quantity demanded" refers to
    (a) Upward shift of the demand curve
    (b) Downward shift of the demand curve
    (c) Movement on the same demand curve
    (d) None of these.

67. An increase in demand can result from
    (a) A decline in market line
    (b) An increase in income
    (c) A reduction in the price of complements
    (d) All of the above.

68. Cross demand is the change in the quantity demanded of a given commodity is responsible to be
    (a) Change in the utility of another commodity
    (b) Change in the price of another commodity
    (c) Change in the price of the nature of another commodity
    (d) Change in the size of another commodity.

69. A normal demand curve slopes down from left to right. This is based on the assumption that
    (a) Price varies directly with quantity demanded
    (b) Marginal utility diminishes as price rises
    (c) There will be power purchases at a higher price than at a lower price
    (d) Income is fixed and so total expenditure in the commodity is limited.

70. Market demand is
    (a) The sum of all individual demands
    (b) Demand at prevailing average prices
    (c) Ability to pay the price asked
    (d) Demand in a perfectly free market.

71. Income distributor affects
    (a) The individual demand for a commodity
    (b) The price of substitutes and complete and complements

(c) The market demand for commodities
(d) The individuals scale at preferences.

72. The shape of an individual demand curve at a given time summarise the relationship between the price a consumer must pay for a given commodity and the quantity of it
(a) That he purchased on previous occasion
(b) That he bought to purchase
(c) That he will purchase
(d) That the commodity might purchase.

73. A commodity the price of which has risen but is expected to become scarce will present a demand curve
(a) Regressive at the lower end
(b) Regressive at the upper end
(c) Linked in the middle
(d) Downward sloping to the right.

74. Extension of demand means
(a) More quantity demanded at a lower price
(b) More quantity demanded at a higher price
(c) More quantity demanded at the same price
(d) None of these.

75. "Market price" is
(a) Short-period equilibrium price
(b) Long-period equilibrium price
(c) Average price in a free market
(d) Average price in all markets.

76. Market demand curve presumes that
(a) All consumers are alike
(b) Incomes of all consumers is the same
(c) Tastes of all consumers are the same
(d) Consumers differ in tastes income and other matters.

77. An income demand curve for an "inferior good" explains:
(a) Initially demand for such goods increases but decreases when income increases beyond a certain level

(b) Demand increases in the same proportion as income increases

(c) Deamnd does not resopond to changes in income

(d) Demand is more than the rate at which income increases.

78. The elasticity of demand describes

(a) The distinction between changes in demand and changes in amount demanded

(b) A changes in the incomes of the buyers in response to change in the prices products they sell

(c) The slope of the demand curve

(d) The responsiveness of price to changes in the quantity demanded

(e) None of the above.

79. To calculate the elasticity of demand which of the following formula is used

(a) Percentage change in demand / original demand

(b) Proportional change in demand / proportional change in price

(c) Change in demand / change in price % original demand / original price

(d) Change in demand / change in price.

80. In measuring price-elasticity

(a) Price is a dependent variable and quantity is an independent variable

(b) Price is an independent variable and quantity is a dependent variable

(c) Price and quantity both are independent variables

(d) Price and quantity both are dependent variables.

81. Income elasticity as demand will be zero when a given change income brings about

(a) A less than proportionate change in quality demanded

(b) A more than proportionate change in quantity demanded

(c) The same proportional change in demand

(d) No change in demand.

82. Demand for a goods is elastic is

(a) Demand for that goods increase when price falls

(b) A price fall produces a decreases in total expenditure in that goods

(c) A price fall produces a less than proportionate rise in the quantity

(d) As a result of a price total expenditure on the goods decreases.

83. In the equation: Price elasticity of demand = ?/ proportionate change price the top line of the fraction should read:

(a) Proportionate change in marginal demand

(b) Increase in quantity demanded

(c) Decrease in aggregrate demand

(d) Proportionate change in quality demanded.

84. Elasticity measures the ratio of changes in quantity demanded to changes in prices expressing both in percentage:

(a) Because it is generally impossible to find data accurate enough to support more precise

(b) Because both measures of change would otherwise be influenced by the units in which they were measured, i.e inches or feet, pounds or ounces, pennies or dollars

(c) For no particular reason, expect that it has become the custom and customs are hard to break

(d) Because in that way there is adjustment for the changing slopes negative throughout with an elasticity of infinity.

85. Is the price elasticity demand for a commodity is less than unity, a decrease in price would result in

(a) A less than proportionate change in the quantity purchased

(b) A more than proportionate change in the quantity purchased

(c) An increase in total expenditure on the product

(d) A shift in the demand curve.

86. A monopolist charging high price operates on
   (a) The elastic part of a deamnd curve
   (b) The inelastic part of a demand curve
   (c) The constant elastic part of a demand curve
   (d) Ignores elaticity of demand altogether.

87. Cross elasticity of demand is measured as:
   (a) Percentage change in the quantity of a commodity demanded divided by percentage change in the price of that commodity
   (b) Percentage change in price of commodity x divided by percentage change in quantity demanded of commodity y
   (c) Percentage change in quantity demanded of commodity x divided by percentage. Change in price of commodity y
   (d) Percentage change in quantity demanded of commodity x divided by percentage change in quantity demanded of commodity y
   (e) Change in price of commodity x divided by change in price of y.

88. Income elasticity of demand is expressed as
   (a) Percentage change in quantity demanded/ percentage change in income
   (b) Percentage change in income/ change in quantity demanded
   (c) Change in quantity demanded x change in marginal income/100
   (d) Change in income/ 100 x change in quantity demanded.

89. Arc elasticity is: proportionate change in the quantity
   (a) Demanded / proportionate change in money income
   (b) In assumption outlay / proportionate change in money income
   (c) Quantity demanded / percentage change in the price
   (d) Change in the price / Original price plus new quantity after change.

90. Cross elasticity of demand is measured as:
    (a) Percentage change in the quantity of a commodity in the price of commodiy
    (b) Percentage change in the quantity demanded of commodity x divided by the percentage change in the price of commodity y
    (c) Change in price of commodity x divided by change in price of x
    (d) Percentage change in the quantity demanded of commodity x divided by the percentage change in the quantity demanded of commodity Y

91. In general, if demand is elastic ,then:
    (a) A price decrease increases total revenue and a price increase decreases total revenue:
    (b) A price decrease decreases total revenue, and a price increases total revenue
    (c) A price increase increases total revenue an da price decrease increases total revenue
    (d) A price increase leaves total revenue unchanged, and so does a price decrease.

92. The shift of a supply curve for a commodity to the left may indicate, other things being equal, that
    (a) Shares in the producing firms are in great demand on the stock exchange
    (b) Producers of the commodity wish to make and sell less at each price
    (c) Prices of raw materials used in the production of the commodity have fallen
    (d) Wages paid to the producers employees have failen.

93. The downward sloping demand curve may be partly explainded by the income effect which refers to
    (a) Peoples tendency to save more as their red incomes fall in the short period
    (b) An increase or decrease in the amount of a good purchased because of a price- included change in the purchasing power of a fixed income

(c) Changes in the relative importance of good purchased because of change in the community's tastes resulting from advertising

(d) Changes in the disribution of income in a community.

94. If more is demanded at the same price or the same quantity is demanded at a higher price, this is known as

(a) Extension of demand (b) Contraction of demand

(c) Increase in demand (d) Decrease in demand.

95. Substitution effect means a consumer

(a) Shifts away from the commodity the price of which has fallen

(b) Shifts in favour of a commodity the price of which has risen

(c) Shifts away from a commodity the price of which has risen and in favour of a commodity the price of which has fallen

(d) None of these.

96. The necessary and sufficient condition for a good to have a positively sloped demand curve is that

(a) The good be inferior

(b) The substitution effect the income effect

(c) The income effect exceed the substitution effect

(d) The good be inferior and the income effect exceed the opposite substitution effect.

97. When the price of a normal goods fall (certeris paribus), more of its is purchased because of

(a) The substitution EFFECT

(b) The income effect

(c) Either the substitution or the income effect

(d) Both the substitution and the income effect.

98. On a linear demand curve the elasticity of demand

(a) Rises up to a point then falls as you move from left to right

(b) Falls steadily as you move from left to right

(c) Rises steadily as you move from left to right

(d) Falls up to point and then rises as you move from left to right.

99. Match the following :

(1) Joint demand	(i)	Tea and coffee
(2) Competitive demand	(ii)	Domestic consumer and industrial users
(3) Composite demand	(iii)	Sugar and massess
(4) Joint supply	(iv)	Lipton tea and Brocke Bond tea
(5) Competitive supply	(v)	Car and petrol

	1	2	3	4	5
(a)	(v)	(iii)	(iv)	(i)	(ii)
(b)	(iv)	(i)	(iii)	(ii)	(v)
(c)	(v)	(i)	(ii)	(iii)	(iv)
(d)	(iii)	(ii)	(iv)	(i)	(v).

100. Match the following:

1	Fall in price	(i)	Demand increase supply unchanged
2.	Rise in price	(ii)	Supply increase demand unchanged
3.	No effect on	(iii)	Supply changes demand unchanged
4.	Rise or fall in price	(iv)	Supply and demand change equally

(a)	(iv)	(iii)	(i)	(ii)
(b)	(ii)	(i)	(iv)	(iii)
(c)	(iv)	(iii)	(ii)	(i)
(d)	(iii)	(i)	(iv)	(ii).

101. Match the following :

1. $\frac{\Delta 9d}{\Delta P}\frac{P}{qd}$ (i) Elasticity of supply

2. $\frac{\Delta q}{\Delta y}\frac{x}{q}$ (ii) Price elasticity of demand

3. $\frac{\Delta qs}{\Delta P} \frac{Py}{qn}$ (iii) Cross elasticity of demand

4. $\frac{\Delta qn}{\Delta Py} \frac{q}{qs}$ (iv) Income elasticity of demand

(a) (iv) (ii) (iii) (i)
(b) (i) (iii) (iv) (ii)
(c) (ii) (iv) (iii) (i)
(d) (iii) (i) (ii) (iv).

102. Match the following :

(1) For a given 10 per cent change in price demand changes by zero per cent (i) E >1

(2) For a given 1- per cent change in price demand changes in price demand changes by 5 per cent (ii) E=1

(3) For a given 10 per cent change in price demand changes by 10 per cent (iii) = e> 1

(4) For a given 10 percent changes in a price demand changes by 20 percent (iv)

(a) (iii) (i) (ii) (iv)
(b) (iv) (iii) (ii) (i)
(c) (i) (ii) (iii) (iv)
(d) (ii) (iii) (i) (iv).

103. Match the following

(1) Responsive of demands to change in price	(i) Income elasticity of demand
(2) Responsive of demand to change in tastes	(ii) Price elasticity of demand
(3) Responsive of demand to change in income	(iii) Cross elasticity of demand
(4) Responsive of demand to demand change in price of related goods	(iv) Taste elasticity of

(a) (i) (ii) (iii) (iv)

(b) (iv) (iii) (i) (ii)

(c) (iii) (iv) (ii) (i)

(d) (ii) (iv) (i) (iii).

104. Match the following :

(1) Positive slope	(i) Demand for sugar
(2) Negative slope	(ii) Demand for inferior goods
(3) Backward slope	(iii) Demand curve
(4) Parallel to income axis	(iv) Supply curve

(a) (i) (iii) (iv) (ii)

(b) (iv) (iii) (ii) (i)

(c) (iv) (i) (ii) (iii)

(d) (ii) (iii) (iv) (i).

105. Match the following:

(1) Increase in quantity with a fall in price	(i) Increase in demand
(2) Increase in quality with a rise in price	(ii) Supply schedule
(3) Fall in price quantity demanded unchanged	(iii) Demand schedule
(4) Rise in price quantity supplied unchanged	(iv) Increase in supply

(a) (i) (iii) (iv) (iii)

(b) (ii) (iii) (iv) (i)

(c) (i) (ii) (iii) (iv)

(d) (iii) (ii) (iv) (i).

106. Which of the following one statements is correc:

(a) Elasticity of demand can vary only between -1.0 and +1.0

(b) Cross elasticity measure the interaction of change in the demand for good A on the price of good B

(c) The demand curves for all commodities which have unitary elastic demand

(d) The demand for all the commodities which have inelastic demand will be vertical lines.

107. Which of the following statements is correct
   (a) When the slope of the demand curve is zero demand is infinity elastic and when the slope is infinite elasticity is zero
   (b) When the slope of the demand curve is zero elasticity is also zero and when the slope is infinite elasticity is also infinite
   (c) When the slope of Re demand curve is zero elasticity is unity and also when the slope is infinite elasticity is unity .
   (d) None of these.

108. Which of the following statements is untrue? Elasticity of supply
   (a) Is a measure of the case with which supply can be increased or decresed
   (b) Tends to way with time
   (c) Is a measure of the responsiveness of supply to changes in price
   (d) Is 1.0 of total revenue is constant to the producer at all levels of output.

109. Which of the following does not have a uniform elasticity of demand at all points?
   (a) A downward sloping demand curve
   (b) A vertical demand curve
   (c) A rectangular hyperbola demand curve
   (d) A horizontal demand curve.

110. Which of the following statements about the elasticity of demand is true ?
   (a) We can tell which produce have close substitutes by their high elasticity of damand
   (b) We can say that necessities have a very low demand elasticity but it largly because we define necessities their very low demand elasticity
   (c) Product sold along with other products are likely to have less elastic demands than product sold alone

(d) Product that are relatively unimportant in terms of total expenditure are likely to have relatively low elasticities of demand

(e) All of these statements are true.

111. Complete the following statements by choosing one of the alternative given below

(a) Equal to one (b) Greater than one

(c) Equal to zero (d) Less than one.

112. Which of following statement is correct

(a) Slope of a curve and its elasticity are one and the same things

(b) Slope of a curve may remain constant elasticity still can and does changes

(c) With a changes in the slope of a curve its elasticity necessarily changes

(d) Two parallel demand curves each cutting the two axis have the same elasticity at a point corresponding to the same price.

113. Which of the follwoing does not have a uniform elasticity of demand at all points ?

(a) A vertical demand curve

(b) A horizontal demand curve

(c) A rectangular hyperbola demand curve

(d) A downward sloping demand curve.

114. The degree of price elasticity of demands used for goods is influenced by whether

1. It has close substitutes
2. It outputs is easily altered
3. It account for a small input
4. It is a durable use or single use goods

(a) 1, 3 and 4 only

(b) 1 and 2 only

(c) 2 and 3 only

(d) 2, 3 and 4 only.

115. Pick out the correct formula for arc elasticity

(a) Q+q1/q1+q x p+p1/p-p1

(b) Q+q1/p-p x q+q1/p+p1

(c) Q-q1/q+q1 x p+p1/p-p1

(d) Q+q1/q-q1 x p+p1/p-p1.

116. The degree pf price elasticity of demand for a good is influenced by whether

1. It is durable use or a single use goods
2. It accounts for a small or large propotion of households total income
3. Its output is easily latered
4. It has close substitutes

(a) 1, 2 and 4 only (b) 1 and 4 only

(c) 2 and 3 only (d) 2, 3 and 4 only

(e) All of them.

117. Which of the following matters may account for changes in demand

1. changes in consumer preferences
2. changes in real incomes
3. changes in distribution of incomes
4. changes in levels of taxation

(a) 1, 2, 3 (b) 2, 3, 4

(c) 1, 3, 4 (d) 1, 2, 3, 4.

118. Which of the following could provide an example of exceptional demand curve

(a) Demand for "Giffen goods"

(b) Demand based on fears of a future rise in price

(c) Demand for second - hand clothes

(d) Demand for daily newspaper.

119. Which of the following one is true incase of normal-goods ?

(a) When price increases demand decreases

(b) When price increases demand also increases

(c) When price remains constant demand fall down

(d) When price fall down demand remains constant.

120. The demand for common salt has low price elasticity because
   (a) It has no close substitutes
   (b) It is a single-use good
   (c) It constitutes only a small proportion pf consumers expenditure
   (d) It can be readily foregone.

ANSWERS

1.	(c)	2.	(c)	3.	(a)	4.	(b)
5.	(d)	6.	(d)	7.	(b)	8.	(b)
9.	(b)	10.	(a)	11.	(c)	12.	(a)
13.	(c)	14.	(a)	15.	(a)	16.	(b)
17.	(c)	18.	(a)	19.	(b)	20.	(b)
21.	(b)	22.	(b)	23.	(c)	24.	(d)
25.	(b)	26.	(b)	27.	(b)	28.	(b)
29.	(a)	30.	(c)	31.	(b)	32.	(a)
33.	(c)	34.	(c)	35.	(c)	36.	(c)
37.	(d)	38.	(c)	39.	(c)	40.	(c)
41.	(b)	42.	(c)	43.	(c)	44.	(d)
45.	(c)	46.	(b)	47.	(a)	48.	(c)
49.	(a)	50.	(b)	51.	(a)	52.	(b)
53.	(b)	54.	(a)	55.	(c)	56.	(c)
57.	(c)	58.	(a)	59.	(c)	60.	(b)
61.	(a)	62.	(d)	63.	(a)	64.	(a)
65.	(c)	66.	(c)	67.	(b)	68.	(b)
69.	(c)	70.	(a)	71.	(c)	72.	(c)
73.	(b)	74.	(a)	75.	(a)	76.	(c)
77.	(a)	78.	(c)	79.	(b)	80.	(b)
81.	(d)	82.	(d)	83.	(d)	84.	(b)
85.	(a)	86.	(b)	87.	(c)	88.	(a)
89.	(d)	90.	(b)	91.	(a)	92.	(d)
93.	(a)	94.	(c)	95.	(c)	96.	(d)
97.	(d)	98.	(b)	99.	(c)	100.	(b)
102.	(c)	103.	(b)	104.	(d)	104.	(b)
106.	(b)	106.	(d)	107.	(c)	108.	(a)
110.	(d)	110.	(c)	111.	(a)	112.	(c)
113.	(d)	114.	(a)	115.	(c)	116.	(a)
117.	(d)	118.	(b)	119.	(b)	120	(a)

6
PUBLIC FINANCE

1. At the end of January 1992 the rate of inflation was
   (a) 11.8% (b) 12.9%
   (c) 13.7% (d) 14.2%.
2. In an open economy the excess of expenditure over domestic borrowing would spill over into
   (a) Fiscal deficit (b) Monetary deficit
   (c) BoP deficit (d) Capital account deficit.
3. The total monetized deficit in 1990-91 stood at
   (a) 2% GDP (b) 2.8% of GDP
   (c) 3.2 % of GDP (d) 1.5 % of GDP.
4. The Budget for 1991-92 was designed to bring down the monetized deficit to
   (a) 2% (b) 1.3%
   (c) 1% (d) None of these.
5. The annual rate of inflation in terms of consumer price index (CPI) for industrial workers during 1990- 91 was
   (a) 13.6% (b) 13%
   (c) 12.6% (d) 12%.
6. According to the Keynesian inflationary gap theory inflationary gap redistribute real income
   (a) In favour of the profit earners
   (b) In favour of the wage earners
   (c) In the exchequer of the Govt
   (d) To none of the above.

7. An inflationary gap map further widen due to
   (a) Keynes effect
   (b) Wealth effect
   (c) Price expectation effect
   (d) All the above.

8. The quantity of money holds that inflation excess due to
   (a) Increases in Govt. expenditure
   (b) Increases in the fiscal deficit
   (c) Lower production of the aggregate level
   (d) Increases in money supply.

9. Inflation implies
   (a) Loss to the debtors (b) Loss to the creditors
   (c) Loss to both (a) and (b) (d) None of the above.

10. During which plan the price level actually declines?
   (a) First (b) Second
   (c) Third (d) Fourth.

11. Bank rate is the rate of which
   (a) A bank lends to the public
   (b) The RBI lends to the public
   (c) The Govt. of India's rate of subsidy
   (d) The RBI extends credit to commercial banks.

12. Who controls the activities of indigenous bankers
   (a) RRBs. (b) Lead Banks
   (c) RBI (d) None of these.

13. The statutory liquidity ratio for commercial banks is
   (a) 20.5% (b) 35%
   (c) 38.5% (d) 40%.

14. Inflation means
   (a) A persistent rise in the general price level
   (b) An increase in the prices of manufactured goods
   (c) An increase in the prices of consumer goods
   (d) An increase in the prices of commodities in a fair price shop.

15. Inflationary gap means excess demand measured at
    (a) Under employment equilibrium level of output
    (b) Dis-equilibrium level of output
    (c) Full-employment level of output
    (d) Over full employment level of output.

16. Ratio of direct to indirect taxes which was 40 : 60 in 1950-51, declined to
    (a) 15:85 in 1991-92 (b) 25:75 in 1991-92
    (c) 30:70 in 1991-92 (d) 35:65 in 1991-92.

17. Indian tax structure indicates that over the year Indian tax system has become increasingly:
    (a) Just (b) Production
    (c) Progressive (d) Unjust.

18. Which of the following is not levied by the central Government?
    (a) Personal income tax
    (b) Corporation tax
    (c) Sales tax
    (d) Custom duties.

19. During the turn of the seventh plan (i.e. 1989-90) sales tax as a percent of state Govt. tax revenue amounted to around
    (a) 39 % (b) 41%
    (c) 43% (d) 45%.

20. Quantitative Credit controls do not include
    (a) Open market (b) Bank rate
    (c) Cash reserve ratio (d) RBI directives.

21. Non-Development expenditure in the current year is projected to rise by about
    (a) 16% (b) 15%
    (c) 14% (d) 13%.

22. The annual plan for 1991-92 provided for a total outlay of
    (a) Rs. 80, 000 (b) Rs. 75, 810 crore
    (c) Rs. 72, 317 crore (d) Rs. 70,200 crore.

23. Of the total outlay for annual plan 1991-92, it was investigated that domestic resources would finance
(a) 80.5% of the outlay (b) 70% of the outlay
(c) 75.5% of the outlay (d) 73% of the outlay.

24. Raja Chelliah Commitee was set up to make proposals on
(a) Banking reform (b) Tax reform
(c) Trade reform (d) Land reform.

25. In 1950-51, the tax income ratio was as low as
(a) 3% (b) 4.5%
(c) 5.4% (d) 6.4%.

26. In 1989-90 the tax income ratio was raised to around
(a) 22% (b) 23%
(c) 24% (d) 25%.

27. In 1991-92, Gross Capital formation reached
(a) 5% (b) 4.7%
(c) 3.7% (d) 3.5%.

28. In 1991-92 outstanding internal liabilities amounted to be around
(a) 52% (b) 53%
(c) 54% (d) 55%.

29. The estimated outstanding external liabilities at the end of 1991-92 stood at
(a) 5.8 % of GDP (b) 4.9 % of GDP
(c) 3.7 % of GDP (d) 2.8% of GDP.

30. The overall budgetary deficit of the centre, state and union territories in 1991-92 is placed at
(a) Rs. 10, 000 crores (b) 10,946 crores
(c) 11,26 crores (d) 12, 000 crores.

31. Development expenditure in the current year is projected to rise by about
(a) 8% (b) 9%
(c) 10% (d) 11%.

32. In the current years budget proposals import duty on captial goods and components was reduced by
    (a) 2 per centage points (P.P)
    (b) 3 P.P
    (c) 4 P.P
    (d) 5 P.P.

33. The additional resource mobilisation measures undertaken in the 1991-92 budget were estimated to yield
    (a) Rs. 2, 616 crore
    (b) Rs. 3,112 crore
    (c) Rs. 3,565 crore
    (d) Rs. 3, 617 crore.

34. A distinct feature of the year's additional resource mobilisation effort is the greater reliance on
    (a) Indirect taxes
    (b) Direct Taxes
    (c) Taxing the NRI deposits
    (d) External sources.

35. The budgetary deficit is sought to be reduced from 2% of GDP in 1990-91 (RE) to
    (a) 1.5% of GDP (b) 1.3 % of GDP
    (c) 1.1 % of GDP (d) 1% of GDP.

36. The central plan outlay of 1991-92 compared to 1990-91 was increased by around
    (a) 13% (b) 12%
    (c) 11% (d) 10%.

37. Reduction in fiscal deficit in 1991-92 involved a fiscal correction of nearly
    (a) Rs. 12000 crore (b) 13,000 crore
    (c) 14,000 crore (d) 14,500 crore.

38. From 1980-81 to 1990-91-GDP ratio has
    (a) Increased (b) Decreased
    (c) Remained constant (d) Become negative.

39. The gap between the revenue GDP ratio and expenditure GDP ratio in 1990-91 was about

(a) 10% (b) 11%
(c) 12% (d) 13%.

40. From 1980-81 to 1990-91 (RE), the direct tax GDP ratio increased from 2.4 % to

(a) 2.5% (b) 3%
(c) 3.5% (d) 4%.

41. During 1981 to 1991, the indirect tax GDP ratio ragistered an increase from 12.2% to

(a) 13.2% (b) 14.3%
(c) 15.4% (d) 16.5%.

42. The voluntary deposits (Immunities and Exemption) Act, 1991 provided an opportunity to the

(a) Tax evaders (b) Small savers
(c) Share holder (d) Pensioners.

43. Under the Income Tax Act, the donation made to AFRICA Fund were made eligible for

(a) 70 % deduction
(b) 80 % deduction
(c) 90 % deduction
(d) 100 % deduction.

44. To encourage the development of a healthy capital market, the basic deduction of taxes in respect of long term capital gain was raised to

(a) Rs. 13,000 (b) Rs.-14,000
(c) Rs. 15,000 (d) Rs. 16,000.

45. Fiscal incentives provided by the Govt. have helped a

(a) Rural bias (b) Labour bias
(c) Capital bias (d) Commercial bias.

46. In recent years, for additional resources, there has been a growing reliance on

(a) Direct taxes (b) Custom duties
(c) Indirect taxes (d) None of these.

47. Interest payment in 1990-91 as a percentage of total expenditure of the centre and increased to nearly

(a) 17% (b) 16%

(c) 15% (d) 14%.

48. In 1990-91, interest payment as a proportion of non-developmental expenditure amount to

(a) 32% (b) 33%

(c) 34% (d) 35%.

49. The proportion of non-developmental expenditure to total expenditure in 1990-91 amounted nearly to

(a) 40 % (b) 42%

(c) 45% (d) 49%.

50. On repartriating Indians stranded in Kuwait during the Gulf Crisis in 1990-91 had to spend

(a) Rs. 250 crore (b) Rs. 290 crore

(c) Rs. 300 crore (d) Rs .310 crore.

51. The revenue deficit-GDP ratio in 1990-91 reached

(a) 3.2 % (b) 3.3%

(c) 3.4% (d) 3.5%.

52. Of the total expenditure of the central Government the interest payment an accumulatecl debt constitutes about

(a) 21 % (b) 22 %

(c) 23 % (d) 24 %.

53. The long term fiscal policy (LTP) document reveals that throughout the 7 Hi plan period the balance from current revenue remained

(a) Zero (b) Positive

(c) Negative (d) Performace budget.

54 The budget presented to Parliament in March 1991 was a

(a) Regular budget

(b) Interim budget

(c) Rail Budget

(d) Performance budget.

55. The regular Budget for 1991-92 envisged a reduction in fiscal deficit to

(a) 5.5 % of GDP (b) 6 % of GDP
(c) 6.5 % Of GDP (d) 7 % of GDP.

56. In 1990-91 fiscal deficit amounted to

(a) 9% of GDP (b) 8.4 % of GDP
(c) 7 % of GDP (d) 7 % of DGP.

57. While calculting personal income tax a rebate is given on

(a) Life Insurance premium
(b) Provident Fund
(c) Both (a) and (b)
(d) Neither on (a) nor in (b).

58. In the budget for 1991-92, the marginal role for income tax has been brought down to

(a) 35 % (b) 40 %
(c) 43 % (d) 45%.

59. Over the years, the degree of progressivity of the Indian tax system has

(a) Remain constant (b) Been increased
(c) Been reduced (d) Become justifiable.

60. Which of the following is not within the income tax net?

(a) Corprtate profit
(b) Personal income above the lowest slab
(c) Agricultural income
(d) Income of the unregistered firm.

61. Estate duty was levied on total property passing

(a) As a gift
(b) On death of a person
(c) On agreement
(d) As a lease.

62. Which of the following taxes was abolished in 1985-

(a) Estate duty (b) Wealth tax
(c) Gift tax (d) Expenditure tax.

63. An annual tax on wealth was first introduced in
(a) 1953 (b) 1957
(c) 1961 (d) 1964.

64. Which of the following is not an indirect tax?
(a) Custom duties (b) Excise duties
(c) Sales tax (d) Corporation tax.

65. An excise duty is levied on
(a) Production
(b) Actual sales
(c) Both Production and Actual
(d) Neither on (a) nor (b).

66. The Indirect Taxation Enquiry Committee was set up in
(a) 1975 (b) 1976
(c) 1777 (d) 1978.

67. Octroi is levied and collected by
(a) Central Govt (b) State Govt
(c) Local bodies (d) All the above.

68. Indirect Taxation Enquiry Committee was set up under the chairmanship of
(a) Manmohan Singh (b) M.L. Dantwala
(c) L.K. Jha (d) Raja Chelliah.

69. A tax which is paid by the person on whom the tax is not incident is called
(a) Indirect tax (b) Direct tax
(c) Local tax (d) Expenditure tax.

70. Put the main source of revenue of the union Govt. in ascending order of importance
(a) Income tax (b) Corporation tax
(c) Customs (d) Excise duties.

71. Which of the following is not on indirect tax ?
(a) Custom duties (b) Land revenue
(c) Entertainment tax (d) Sales tax.

72. Amount given by the govt or by the private body to encourage a particular economic acitivity is called
(a) Subsidy (b) Grant
(c) Loan (d) Mutal Funds.

73. All taxes come under
(a) Revenue receipts (b) Capital receipts
(c) Public dept (d) Both (a) and (b).

74. Investment in public works is known as
(a) Revenue expenditure (b) Current expenditure
(c) Capital expenditure (d) Both (B) and (C).

75. Non-development expenditure involves
(a) Defence (b) Interest payments
(c) Irrigation (d) Subsidies.

76. The most important cause of the rapidly rising prices is the heavy reliance of the croxt on
(a) Deficit financing
(b) Borrowing funds from the public
(c) Borrowing funds from the IMF
(d) Credit facilities from the RBI.

77. An any points of time, the supply of money reform to its
(a) Stock (b) Flow
(c) Stock as well as flow (d) Currency flexibility.

78. The stock of money always to the stock of money
(a) Held by the public
(b) Held by the private sector
(c) Held by the government of India
(d) Held by the RBI and ather commercial banks.

79. According to the definitions of the RBI, there are
(a) Two- measures of money supply
(b) Three measures of M.S.
(c) Four measures of M.S.
(d) Five measures of M.S..

80. Currency held by the public + net demand deposits of banks + other deposits of the R.B.I. is defined as

(a) M_1 (b) M_2
(c) M_3 (d) M_4.

81. M_2 is defined as

(a) M_1+ net time deposits of banks
(b) M_1+ saving deposits with post office saving banks
(c) Both (a) and (b)
(d) Neither (a) nor (b).

82. M_3 is defined as

(a) C+DD+OD+ net time deposits of banks
(b) C+OD+OD+national saving certificate
(c) M_4+-M_1
(d) M_1+ saving deposits with post office savings bank.

83. M_4 is defined as

(a) M_3- M_1
(b) M_1+M_1+M_2
(c) M_3+ total deposits with the post office saving organisation (excluding NCC)
(d) M_1+net fiscal defcits of the govt.

84. In 1990-91, broad money (M_3) growth turned out to be around

(a) 15 % (b) 16 %
(c) 17 % (d) 18 %.

85. M_3 growth is lower in 1990-91 compared to 1989-90 because of

(a) Low fiscal deficit
(b) Low monetary policy
(c) BoP crisis
(d) Low savings rate.

86. During 1991-92 reserve money expended to be around

(a) 17 % (b) 16 %
(c) 15 % (d) 14 %.

87. The economic realities dicated the adoption of
    (a) Open monetary policy
    (b) Restrictive monetary policy
    (c) Using both (a) and (b)
    (d) Inflexible monetary policy.

88. Consistent with output and inflation target, M_3 growth has been target at
    (a) 17 % (b) 15 %
    (c) 13 % (d) 11 %.

89. On May 4, 1991 the incremental gas Reserve requiement has been imposed to
    (a) 10 % (b) 11 %
    (c) 13 % (d) 14 %.

90. The growth rate of M_1 has been higher in the financial year than that of M_3 because of a
    (a) Much larger rise in demand deposits than time deposits.
    (b) Much larger rise in time deposits than demand deposits
    (c) Rise in both time and demand deposits
    (d) Fall in both the time and demand deposits.

91. In the current financial year, demand deposits with the bank has recorded a growth of
    (a) 20 % (b) 25.5%
    (c) 27% (d) 30.5%.

92. Net bank credit to Govt. during 1991-92 recorded a growth of around
    (a) 17% (b) 18%
    (c) 19% (d) 20%.

93. Which of the following accounts for the lions share of the increase in reserve money
    (a) Net RBI credit to government
    (b) Net RBI credit to commercial banks
    (c) Net RBI credit to the co-operative institution
    (d) Net RBI credit to industrial reconstruction.

94. The bank rate in the current financial year has been revised twice from 10 % to

(a) 11% (b) 12%
(c) 13% (d) 14%.

95. The monetary policy in 1991-92 was restrictive to contain

(a) The growth of Monetary demand
(b) The growth of money supply
(c) The growth of aggregate demand
(d) The growth of imports.

96. The prescribed cash margin on imports under OG2 other than Capital goods has been raised to

(a) 150 % (b) 170%
(c) 200% (d) 210%.

97. Which one of the following is not a money market instrument

(a) 182 days treasury bills
(b) Certificates of deposit (CDS)
(c) Commercial papers (CPs)
(d) Shares and dontores.

98. Commercial paper (CPs) as a menetary instrument was introduced in

(a) 1989 (b) 1990
(c) 1991 (d) 1992.

99. Which of the following banks do not fall within the purview of the Indian Banking Regulation Act 1949

(a) State Bank of India
(b) Reserve Bank of India
(c) Hong-Kong Bank operating in India
(d) Co-operative Bank.

100. The call money market is also known as

(a) Inter bank call money market
(b) The treasury bill market
(c) The commercial bill market
(d) The commercial paper market.

101. Who plays an important rate in the call money market?
   (a) Money lenders (b) Share holders
   (c) Brokers (d) None of the above.

102. Treasury Bills are
   (a) Very short term liability of the Govt.
   (b) Short term liability of the Govt.
   (c) Medium term liability of the Govt.
   (d) Long term liability of the Govt.

103. Of the total outstanding treasury Bills RBI holds almost
   (a) 90% (b) 80%
   (c) 70% (d) 60%.

104. The certificates of deposits (CD) can be issued only by the
   (a) Non bank financial institutions
   (b) Reserve Bank of India
   (c) Scheduled Commercial Bank
   (d) Co-operative banks.

105. Maturity period of CD ranged from
   (a) 3 moths to 6 monthes
   (b) 7 months to 11 months
   (c) 8 months and 12 months
   (d) 1 months to 2 months.

106. The commercial paper (CP) can be issued by a listed company which has a net of at least Rs. 10 crcres and a working capital of not less than
   (a) Rs. 25 crores (b) Rs. 30 crores
   (c) Rs. 35 crores (d) Rs. 40 crores.

107. Reserve Bank of India became a state owned Institution in the year
   (a) 1935 (b) 1947
   (c) 1949 (d) 1951.

108. As on June 30, 1991 the State Bank of India had
   (a) 9000 branches (b) 84,62 branches
   (c) 7898 branches (d) 7500 branches.

109. Before July 1, 1955, State Bank of India was known as
   (a) National Bank of India
   (b) Central Bank of India
   (c) Commercial Bank of India
   (d) Imperial Bank of India.

110. The Lead Bank Scheme was formulated in the year
   (a) 1967 (b) 1968
   (c) 1969 (d) 1970.

111. The National Credit Council is
   (a) An advisory body (b) A supervisory body
   (c) A Statutory body (d) A promotional body.

112. Aggregated bank deposits by the nationalised banks at the end of 1991 were
   (a) Rs 2,20,000 crore (b) Rs 2,29,748 crore
   (c) Rs 2,18,111 crore (d) Rs 2,15,200 crore.

113. By December 27, 1991, the credit deposits stood at
   (a) 54.4% (b) 57.9%
   (c) 58% (d) 60.1 %.

114. Credit Authorisation scheme was introduced in
   (a) 1963 (b) 1964
   (c) 1965 (d) 1968.

115. National Credit Council was set up in
   (a) 1965 (b) 1966
   (c) 1967 (d) 1968.

116. Of the total increase in gross bank credit in the two years 1989-90 and 1990-91 industry accounted for
   (a) 38.3% (b) 39.1%
   (c) 40% (d) 42.5%.

117. Legal tender in India includes
   (a) Notes issued by RBI
   (b) Notes issued by Finance Ministry
   (c) Coins and bank notes
   (d) Gold coins.

118. The central banking function in India is performed by
   (a) The Central Bank of India
   (b) State Bank of India
   (c) Reserve Bank of India
   (d) Ministry of finance.

119. The functions of RBI are:
   1. Issuing all notes and coins
   2. Distributing all notes and coins
   3. Formulating monetary policy
   4. Acting as agent of Govt.
   (a) 1, 3, 4 (b) 2, 3, 4
   (c) 2 and 3 (d) 1, 2, 3, 4.

120. Which of the following is not correct about the voluntary deposits scheme?
   (a) Any person could make deposit with NHB
   (b) Such bank could credit 40 % of such deposit
   (c) The depositor could utilize freely the remaining net deposit
   (d) The net deposit is taxable.

121. A custom duty is exempted for the import of the capital goods designed to the
   (a) Development of software for export
   (b) Promotion of agricultural technology
   (c) Development of indigenous capability in industries
   (d) Development of small scale industries.

122. Among the third world countries, India is one of the
   (a) Lowest taxed countries
   (b) Highest taxed countries
   (c) Moderately taxed countries
   (d) Indiscriminately taxed countries.

123. A reduction in the rate of taxation leads to more than proportionate increase in tax yield' a theory related to
   (a) Laffer curve
   (b) The curve phenomenon

(c) Marshall-Lerner condition

(d) Mezier's paradox.

124. The long-term fiscal policy stressed the need for strengthening the

(a) Consumption incentives

(b) Saving incentives

(c) Propensity to import the capital goods

(d) Public sectors rate in-economic development.

125. In order to make direct tax system more effective, the Raja Chelliah Committee recommended

(a) Higher rates of taxation

(b) The taxation rate at par with the developed countries

(c) Lower rate of taxation

(d) The rate of taxation at the poor with the other LDC's.

126. Under the constitution, the power to raise and diburse public funds

(a) Has been vested in the union govt.

(b) Is divided between the union and state govt.

(c) Has been vested upon Finance Commission

(d) Has been vested upon the Ministry of finance.

127. The conventional budgetary deficit is the difference between

(a) All receipts and expenditure

(b) All expenditure and receipts

(c) Government loans and credits recovered

(d) Government asset and liabitities.

128. The revenue deficit denotes the difference between

(a) Revenue expenditure and revenue receipts

(b) Revenue receipts and revenue expenditure

(c) RBI's debt and credit account

(d) Net government surplus on monetary receipts.

129. Monetary deficit is the

(a) Government deficit on payments disbursement

(b) RBI's deficit due to outstanding dues
(c) Net RBI credit to the central government
(d) Difference between government payments and receipts in monetary term.

130. Gross fiscal deficit is the
(a) Excess of total govt. expenditure over revenue receipts and grants
(b) Total of Govt's non plan expenditure
(c) Difference between govt's non planned and planned expenditure
(d) Difference between non developmental expenditure and capital gain.

131. The budget for 1991-92, invisaged a reduction in the fiscal deficit by
(a) One percentage point of GDP
(b) Two percentage point of GDP
(c) Three percentage point of GDP
(d) Four percentage point of GDP.

132. Most of the reduction in fiscal deficit in 1991-92 was sought to be achieved through reduction in
(a) Planned expenditure (b) Non-plan expenditure
(c) Interest payment (d) Pension payments.

133. Which of the following is not a part of the policy initiatives introduced in the budget to reduce fiscal deficit?
(a) Reduction in fertiliser subsidy
(b) Abolition of CCS for export
(c) Abolition of subsidy on sugar distributed through the PDS
(d) Abolition of pension payments.

134. During the 80'c revenue GDP ratio of India has
(a) Increased
(b) Decreased
(c) Remained Constant
(d) Became almost insignificant.

135. Prudent fiscal management demands that revenue deficits should not only meet revenue expenditure but also a surplus for meeting.
   (a) Capital expenditure
   (b) Budgetary expenditure
   (c) Government liabilities
   (d) Interest rate payments.

136. In the fiscal management of 1991-92, measures in the field of direct taxes were targeted at reversing the
   (a) Declining trend in tax revenue share
   (b) Increasing trend in tax revenue share
   (c) Constancy in the tax revenue share
   (d) Negatively in the tax revenue share.

137. Which one of the following is not an objectives of changes in indirect tax regime?
   (a) Reducing excessive reliance on custom duties
   (b) Ensuring price-stability for essential commodities
   (c) Curbing conspicuous consumption
   (d) Increasing the indirect taxes revenue more than doubled than the past ten level.

138. Government announced the voluntary deposits communities and exemptions) scheme to mobilise
   (a) Saving out of family income
   (b) Captial from surplus to the scarce units
   (c) Unaccounted money
   (d) Savings out of corporate profits.

139. The schemes viz. remittance in Foreign Exchange communities scheme, 1991 and India Development Bond 1991, were announced to tackle the
   (a) Inflow of remittances from the Gulf countries
   (b) Problems of development in the capital market
   (c) Interest rate payments on foreign bans
   (d) Balance of payment problem.

140. The scope of expenditure tax has been extended to cover
   (a) Tea and beverages from local hotel
   (b) Food and Drink's from AC restaurants
   (c) Pan-masala and soft drinks
   (d) Staying in five star hotels.

141. The gap between assets and liabilities of the central government reflects deficit on:
   (a) Capital account (b) Current account
   (c) Revenue account (d) Savings account.

ANSWERS

1.	(a)	2.	(c)	3.	(b)	4.	(b)
5.	(a)	6.	(d)	7.	(a)	8.	(d)
9.	(b)	10.	(a)	11.	(d)	12.	(d)
13.	(a)	14.	(a)	15.	(c)	16.	(a)
17.	(d)	18.	(c)	19.	(a)	20.	(d)
21.	(c)	22.	(c)	23.	(a)	24.	(b)
25.	(d)	26.	(a)	27.	(b)	28.	(a)
29.	(a)	30.	(b)	31.	(a)	32.	(d)
33.	(a)	34.	(b)	35.	(b)	36.	(a)
37.	(a)	38.	(a)	39.	(d)	40.	(a)
41.	(b)	42.	(a)	43.	(d)	44.	(c)
45.	(c)	46.	(c)	47.	(d)	48.	(d)
49.	(a)	50.	(c)	51.	(b)	52.	(d)
53.	(c)	54.	(b)	55.	(c)	56.	(b)
57.	(c)	58.	(b)	59.	(c)	60.	(c)
61.	(b)	62.	(a)	63.	(b)	64.	(d)
65.	(a)	66.	(b)	67.	(c)	68.	(c)
69.	(a)	70.	(a)	71.	(b)	72.	(a)
73.	(a)	74.	(c)	75.	(a)	76.	(a)
77.	(a)	78.	(a)	79.	(c)	80.	(a)
81.	(b)	82.	(a)	83.	(c)	84.	(a)
85.	(c)	86.	(c)	87.	(b)	88.	(c)
89.	(a)	90.	(b)	91.	(b)	92.	(a)
93.	(a)	94.	(b)	95.	(c)	96.	(c)
97.	(d)	98.	(b)	99.	(d)	100.	(a)
101.	(c)	102.	(b)	103.	(a)	104.	(c)

105.	(a)	106.	(a)	107.	(c)	108.	(b)
109.	(d)	110.	(c)	111.	(a)	112.	(b)
113.	(a)	114.	(c)	115.	(d)	116	(a)
117.	(c)	118.	(c)	119.	(b)	120.	(a)
121.	(a)	122.	(b)	123.	(a)	124.	(b)
125.	(c)	126.	(b)	127.	(a)	128.	(b)
129.	(c)	130.	(a)	131.	(b)	132.	(b)
133.	(d)	134.	(c)	135.	(a)	136	(a)
137.	(d)	138.	(c)	139.	(d)	140.	(b)
141	(c)						

7
INDIAN AGRICULTURE

1. In 1950-51, the share of agriculture in GDP was
   (a) 40 per cent
   (b) 50 per cent
   (c) Above 55 per cent
   (d) Less than 55 per cent.

2. The share of agriculture in 1989-90 (at 1980-81 prices) had been around
   (a) 40 per cent of GDP (b) 45% of GDP
   (c) 46% of GDP (d) 50% of GDP.

3. The percentage of population engaged in agriculture in 1950-51 was about
   (a) 70% (b) 65%
   (c) 60% (d) 59%.

4. The largest employment providing sector is
   (a) Industry (b) Agriculture
   (c) Commerce (d) Small scale sector.

5. The share of agriculture in total export in 1990-91 was around
   (a) 16% (b) 17%
   (c) 18% (d) 19%.

6. The case of disguised unemployment in agriculture occurs when the worker's marginal productivity on land becomes
   (a) Zero (b) One
   (c) Infinity (d) None of these.

7. According to National Sample Survey, income elasticity of demand for foodgrain in India is

(a) 0.8 (b) 0.7
(c) 0.6 (d) 0.5.

8. Planning Commission has estimated that demand for agricultural commodity is likely to increase at the rate of

(a) 4.7% per annum (b) 5% per annum
(c) 5.6 %per annum (d) 6% per annum.

9. According to Planning Commission, India can achieve self reliant in agriculture if agricultural output rises at the rate of

(a) 4% (b) 5%
(c) 6% (d) 7%.

10. Over per lakh hectares of gross cropped area in 1950-51, there were only

(a) 9 Tractors (b) 8 Tractors
(c) 7 Tractors (d) 6 Tractors.

11. In 1951-52, the percentage of foodgrain production that went to the farmers own cosumption was approximately

(a) 45 (b) 49
(c) 50 (d) 51.

12. At the time of Independence, the percentange of land area under the Zamindari system was about

(a) 60 (b) 59
(c) 58 (d) 57.

13. Total net shown area in 1950-51 was about

(a) 110 million hectares
(b) 119 million hectares
(c) 120 million hectares
(d) 121 million hectares.

14. The net irrigated area in 1950-51 was only about

(a) 21 million hectares (b) 18 millian hectares
(c) 15 million hectares (d) 13 million hectares

15. Western Rajasthan and a part of the Thar desert have a very uncertain rainfall of

(a) 6 to 7 inches (b) 4 to 5 inches
(c) 2 to 3 inches (d) 1 to 2 inches.

16. Cherrapunji in Assam has an annual reainfal about

(a) 450 inches (b) 500 inches
(c) 525 inches (d) 530 inches.

17. The entire cultivated area of the country suffers from the deficiency of

(a) Urea (b) Nitrogen
(c) Super phosphate (d) None of the above.

18. Cropping pattern in India is determined mainly by

(a) Natural factors (b) External factors
(c) The availability of fertilisers (d) Internal factor.

19. The most important foodgrain crop in India is

(a) Wheat (b) Rice
(c) Bazra (d) Millets.

20. After 1984, in almost all states, the area under wheat was approximately

(a) 18% (b) 20%
(c) 19% (d) 21%.

21. From 1950-51 to 1990-91, the area under oilseeds has increased from 10.7 million hectares to

(a) 21.7 million hectares (b) 23 million hectares
(c) 23.5 million hectares (d) 24 million hectares.

22.. The cropping pattern in India is

(a) unbalanced (b) Balanced
(c) Stable (d) Unspecified.

23. The area under pulses between 1951 and 1991 has

(a) Increased
(b) Decreased
(c) Remained Constant
(d) Not been determined.

24. In the Index number of agricultural production, sugarcane carries a weight of

(a) 8 (b) 7
(c) 6 (d) 5.

25. During 1990-91, foodgrains production reached.

(a) 176 million tonnes (b) 172 million tonnes
(c) 180 million tonnes (d) 181 million tonnes.

26. The irrigation potential estimated to have created by 1990-91 was about:

(a) 84 million hectares (b) 83 m.n.
(c) 81 m.n. (d) 80 m.n..

27. In 1990-91, fertilizer consumption reached approximately

(a) 16 million tonnes (b) 15 m.t.
(c) 14 m.t. (d) 13 m.n..

28. Fertilizer subsidy during 1990-91 amounted to

(a) Rs. 4389 crores (b) Rs. 4350 crores
(c) Rs. 4345 crores (d) Rs. 4340 crores.

29. As a fiscal correction, the Union Budget for 1991-92 increased issue process of fertilisers by

(a) 27% (b) 28%
(c) 2 9% (d) 30%.

30. During 1990-91, milk production is estimated to have

(a) 54 million tonnes (b) 55 m.t.
(c) 56 m.t. (d) 57 .T.

31. The target level of foodgrains productions during 1991-92 is

(a) 180 m.t. (b) 181 m.t.
(c) 182 m.t. (d) 183 m.t..

32. Integrated programme for rice development covers

(a) 23 states
(b) 24 states
(c) 25 states
(d) 25 states and one Union Territory.

33. For 1991-92, the target level of the rice production has fixed to

(a) 77.5 m.t (b) 77 m.t
(c) 76.5 m.t (d) 76 m.t.

34. Between 1950-51 and 1990-91 the productivity of wheat has increased by

(a) 3.4 times (b) 3 times
(c) 2.5 times (d) 2 times.

35. Which of the following is a coarse grain?

(a) Rice (b) Wheat
(c) Soybean (d) Barley.

36. For pulses the percentage of the area under irrigation is about

(a) 19% (b) 17%
(c) 12% (d) 9%.

37. The production of pulses in 1991-92 has been targetted at

(a) 20 m.t. (b) 17.5m.t.
(c) 15.5 m.t (d) 14 m.t.

38. The oilseeds production programme in 1991-92 is operating in

(a) 15 states (b) 16 states
(c) 17 states (d) 18 states.

39. In 1991-92, the production of oilseeds has been targeted of

(a) 18.5 m.t (b) 19 m.t
(c) 19.5 m.t (d) 20 m.t.

40. Sugarance prodution in 1990-91 reached a level of

(a) 250 m.t (b) 247.7 m.t
(c) 240.3 m.t (d) 239 m.t.

41. Which one of the following is a horticultural crop?

(a) Ground nut (b) Cashewnut
(c) Soybean (d) Millets.

42. To encourage for its development, coconut has been declared as
    (a) Horticulture crop
    (b) Plantation crop
    (c) Oilseed crop
    (d) Commercial crop.

43. From the total export earnings from spices, pepper accounts for about
    (a) 70% (b) 80%
    (c) 85% (d) 90%.

44. Of the total tea output, domestic market takes about
    (a) 1/3rd (b) 2/3rd
    (c) 1/2rd (d) 1/2.

45. The target for the tea exports for 1991-92 has been fired at
    (a) 180 million k.g. (m.k) (b) 190 m.k
    (c) 190 m.k (d) 210 m.k.

46. The domestic consumption of coffee is stable would
    (a) 50,000 tonnes (b) 55,0000 tonnes
    (c) 60,0000 tones (d) 65, 000 tones.

47. The highest rubber growing states in India is
    (a) Kerala (b) Tamil Nadu
    (c) Andhra Pradesh (d) Orissa.

48. The most crucial factor influencing agricultureal production is
    (a) Irrigation (b) Institutional support
    (c) Credit facility (d) Monsoon.

49. Which of the following fall under ground water scheme?
    (a) Tanks (b) Reservoirs
    (c) Streams (d) Wells.

50. National Water Resources Council was set up in
    (a) 1983 (b) 1984
    (c) 1985 (d) 1986.

51. National water policy accorded highest priority to
   (a) Irrigation
   (b) Drinking water
   (c) Ground water
   (d) Pollution control of the river water.

52. In 1990-91, HYV (high yielding variety) programme had covered arround
   (a) 64 million hectares (b) 65 m.h
   (c) 64 m.h (d) 66 m.h.

53. In 1991-92, the consumption of fertilizers is expected to be around
   (a) 14 million tonnes (b) 15 m.t.
   (c) 16 m.t. (d) 17 m.t.

54. Fertilizer retention price and subsidy scheme was introduced in
   (a) 1976 (b) 1977
   (c) 1978 (d) 1979.

55. Consumption of pesticides in 1990-91 is estimated to be of
   (a) 82,000 tonnes
   (b) 80,000 tonnes
   (c) 75,000 tonnes
   (d) 70,000 tonnes.

56. The target fixed for the consumption of pesticides in 1991-92 is
   (a) 82,500 tonnes (b) 83,000 tonnes
   (c) 84,000 tonnes (d) 85,000 tonnes.

57. In 1981, the institutional sources of rural credit amounted to
   (a) 50 per cent (b) 53 per cent
   (c) 61 per cent (d) 70 per cent.

58. The most important non-institutional sources of rural credit is the
   (a) Landlord (b) Money lender
   (c) Managing agency (d) Relatives.

59. The National Bank for Agriculture and Rural Development was set up in

(a) 1982 (b) 1983

(c) 1984 (d) 1985.

60. The cooperative movement in India was initiated in

(a) 1901 (b) 1904

(c) 1907 (d) 1909.

61. Regional rural banks (RRB) was set up in

(a) 1973 (b) 1974

(c) 1975 (d) 1976.

62. Of the total rural credits in 1951-52, co-operatives provided only

(a) 3.1% (b) 4.2%

(c) 5.3% (d) 6%.

63. Co-operatives in India have a

(a) Two-tier structure

(b) Three-tier structure

(c) Forth-tier structure

(d) Unified structure.

64. Share of commercial banks in rural credit during 1951-52 was only

(a) 0.9% (b) 2%

(c) 3.3% (d) 4%.

65. How many commercial Banks were nationalised in 1969?

(a) 17 (b) 16

(c) 15 (d) 14.

66. By the turn of the century, the direct demand for rural credit is estimated to be of

(a) Rs. 1,10,873 crores (b) Rs. 1,11,579 crores

(c) Rs. 1,12,111, crores (d) Rs. 1, 13,121 crores.

67. 'Operation Flood' is related to

(a) Flood Control (b) Construction of dams

(c) Dairy development (d) None of the above.

68. During eighth plan, special emphasis in agricultural development is being envisaged in the
 (a) Northern region (b) Southern region
 (c) Eastern region (d) Western region .

69. During 1990-91 co-operatives marketed agricultural produce of the value of
 (a) Rs. 5000 crores (b) Rs. 5, 100 crores
 (c) Rs. 5, 400 crores (d) Rs. 5, 600 crores.

70. Which one of the following is the failure of efforts to improve agricultural production?
 (a) Low yield per area
 (b) Non-reclamation of barren land
 (c) Very little development of irrigation facilities
 (d) None of these.

71. Which of the following measures can be taken to modernise agricultural sector?
 (a) Development of transport system
 (b) Development of rural industries
 (c) Social welfare service
 (d) Community development.
 (e) All of these

72. Which of the following measures have been taken to modernise Indian agriculture?
 (a) Area under irrigation increased
 (b) High yielding variety seeds
 (c) Credit facilities to villages
 (d) All of these.

73. Which of the following factors is not responsible for the low productivity in agriculture in India?
 (a) Use of primitive equipment
 (b) Financial weakness of the farmers
 (c) Uneconomic size of holdings?
 (d) Development on monsoons

(e) Lack of fertilizers.

74. Fiscal policy in India has as on a objectives
(a) Regressive taxation
(b) Establishment of a welfare state
(c) Management of public debt
(d) All the above.

75. The states debt does not include
(a) Loans from the SBI
(b) Loans from line union govt.
(c) Provident funds
(d) Treasury bills issued to international financial industries.

76. The low productivity of agriculture in India is not caused by
(a) Inadequate availability of inputs
(b) Subdivision of land holdings
(c) Less area under cultivation
(d) Poor finance facilities.

77. Agricultural marketing in India has certain defects which do not include
(a) Inadequate transport facilities
(b) Lack of standard measures and weights
(c) Agricultural produce not being properly graded
(d) Insufficient price incentives by the government.

78. The measures taken by the government in the field of agricultural marketing do not include
(a) Elimination of middlemen
(b) Setting up of regulated markets
(c) Grading and standardisation
(d) Dissemination of market information.

79. Which of the following collects and publishes the latest information about agricultural markets.
(a) Directorate of Economics and Statistics
(b) Directorate of Marketing and Inspection

(c) Food Corporation of India
(d) National Council of Applied Economic Research.

80. The increase in agricultural production is due to
(a) Increase in area under crops
(b) Improvement in yield
(c) Improvement in cropping pattern
(d) Effective implementation of land reforms.
1. (a) and (c) 2. (a) and (b)
3. (a) (b) and (c) 4. 1, 2, 3 and 4

81. India is primarily an agricultural economy because:
(a) Indian agriculture has not been nationalised
(b) India lacks basic and key industries
(c) India has opened more banks in rural areas
(d) All of the above.

82. The total work-force engaged in agriculture and allied activities forms about
(a) One-third of the total labour Force
(b) Two-third of the total labour Force
(c) One-half of the total labour Force
(d) One-Fourth of the total labour Force.

83. Intensive agriculture forms an integral point of agriculture development strategy in India. By intensive agriculture we mean
(a) Reclamation of barren land
(b) Reclamation of water-logged land
(c) Making use of better agriculture technology to raise the productivity of land
(d) Reclamation of sea.

84. Slow progress of Indian agriculture cannot be attributed to
(a) Inadequate irrigation
(b) Slow spread of new technology
(c) Slow growth of Industries
(d) Defective land system.

85. By package programme we mean

(a) Packing of all agricultural produce ina big countainer for marketing whole sale

(b) Packing of all agricultural produce in a small container for marketing retail

(c) Using togther all agricultural input for raising production

(d) Using all output and input in the form of packets:.

86. Mechanisation of agriculture of India is advocated on the ground that

(a) It will rise agricultural activity

(b) Small form predominate in India, hence the cost of mechanisation on the small farm will be low

(c) Animal power will become superfluous

(d) Human power can be shifted to other more productive uses.

87. Following steps can be taken to ensure that the small and marginal farmers are brought within the ambit of Green Revolution

(a) Small farmers should be given adequate credit facilities

(b) Small farmer should be encouraged to join cooperatives

(c) Small farmer should be supplied farm-machines on their purchase basis

(d) All of the above.

88. By Green Revolution, as its has happend in India, we largely mean

(a) Large increase in the area devoted to the cultivation of wheat

(b) Large increase in the area devoted to the cultivation of all crops including wheat

(c) Large increase in the area devoted to the cultivation of all food crops including rice and wheat

(d) Large increase in production of foodgrains which took place in a short span of time.

89. Green Revolution has not been filled that 'Green' as it has been made out to because
   (a) It is confined mainly to wheat and rice
   (b) It is confined to select regions
   (c) Land reform remain unimplemented
   (d) Consumption of fertilizers has not picked up.

90. A defective agricultural marketing system works as a barrier to economic growth in general because
   (a) It enriches large farmer at the expence of small farmer and thus saving suffer in the economy
   (b) It raises the price of that the final consumers have to pay for the product since a large chain of middle man will pocket profits for themselves
   (c) It work as a disincentive to the transport and communication network
   (d) It work as a disincentive to the farmers to sell in the markets and thus reduce the size of the market surplus.
   (e) All of the above

91. In the eighties India's agriculture production showed
   (a) An increase in all crops
   (b) An increase mainly in wheat, paddy, sugarcane and potatoes only
   (c) An increase mainly in jowar, gram, oilseeds
   (d) An increase in none of these crops.

92. The major achievements in the agriculture sector during the Five Year Plan do not include
   (a) Initiation of the Green Revolution
   (b) Continuing increase in irrigation facilities
   (c) Rising number of farmers benefiting from land reforms
   (d) Rising number of people living below the poverty line.

93. Absentee landlordism means that
   (a) The landlord cuts off all high links with his land
   (b) The landlord temporarily stays away from land leaving it cultivated

(c) The landlord lets out his holding and claims a share of the produce in the form of rent

(d) The landlord transfers all his proprietory rights to the cultivator.

94. By land reforms we mean

(a) Improvement in agrarian relations

(b) Enlargement of the size of small units of cultivation

(c) Improvement in agrarian relations and also enlargement of the size of small units of cultivation

(d) None of the above.

95. Agriculture contributes to industrial development

(a) By earning foreign exchange

(b) By making available resource for over-head investment and expansion secondary industries

(c) By raising cash income to stimulate demand for industrial product

(d) By supplying food and raw materials

(e) All of the above.

96. Which of the following measures have been adopted to modernise Indian agriculture

(a) Use of HYV seeds

(b) Expansion in area under irrigation

(c) Adequate supply of credit

(d) Extensive use of fertilizers

(e) All of the above.

97. The major reasons for the spread of Green Revolution only to a few crops are

(a) Urgent necessity of devoting more attention to foodgrains

(b) Heavy industry-based strategy adopted in our plans required a substantial step up in the basic wage good, viz. foodgrain

(c) Slow growth of HYV seeds in case of others crops

(d) All of the above.

98. By ceiling on holdings as presently defined in India we mean that
    (a) A family cannot own land beyond the prescribed maximum
    (b) An individual cannot own land beyond that prescribed maximum.
    (c) A family cannot cultivate land beyond the prescribed maximum
    (d) An individual cannot cultivate land beyond the prescribed maximum

99. The most effective aspects of Indian agriculture scheme in recent years have been
    (a) Fertilisers, credit, irrigation, research and new varieties of seeds
    (b) Manures, power, land reformrs and intensive farming
    (c) Price support, government help, storage, and transportation
    (d) Transportation, agriculture education, communication and extension.

100. Two basic objectives of land reforms in India are:
    (a) To increase the area under irrigation and fertilisers
    (b) To facilitate in opening of rural bajks and ware houses
    (c) To stabilise the prices of agriculture and industrial goods
    (d) To promote growth and social justice in the agrarian economy.

101. Land reforms is needed because
    (a) Under present arrangement farmers have little incentive to improve productivity
    (b) Output levels will unquestionably rise
    (c) There is grave inequality in the distribution of land
    (d) Both (a) and (c).

102. In view of the present somewhat easy position in respect of production and stocks of foodgrains what is immediately required is

(a) To take steps to promote further the level of production
(b) To take steps to remove transport bottlenecks in food deficit area
(c) To take step to achieve price stability
(d) All of the above.

103. The target for foodgrains production for 1989-90 as laid down in the seventh plan 1985-90 was
(a) 178.0 to 183 million tonnes
(b) 144.5 to 149.5 million tonnes
(c) 149.5 to 154.5 million tonnes
(d) 154.5 to 159.5 million tonnes.

104. The seventh plan 1985-90 projected the foodgrain requirements for 1989-90 at
(a) 140.48 to 144.48 million tonnes
(b) 164.80 to 169.0 million tonnes
(c) 174.07 to 181.32 million tonnes
(d) 179.50 to 185.50 million tonnes.

105. The National Agriculture Credit Fund step up by the Reserve Bank of India extends
(a) Short-term loan to agriculture
(b) Medium-term
(c) Long-term
(d) Medium and long term loan to agriculture.

106. The Reserve Bank of India provides
(a) Direct finance to agriculture
(b) Refinance
(c) Direct short term finance to agriculture
(d) Direct loan.

107. At the village level, the loan from the cooperative institution are disbursed by the
(a) Primary Agriculture Credit Societies
(b) The Central Cooperative Bank
(c) The State Cooperative Bank
(d) The NABARD.

108. Government measure to solve the food problem have been concerned with

   (a) Distribution of foodgrain
   (b) Price fixation of foodgrain
   (c) Demand for foodgrain
   (d) All of the above.

109. One of the following is not a factor determines the size of economic holding. Which?

   (a) Farming techniques and practices
   (b) Social condition relating to the status of land-ownership
   (c) Geographical and climatic condition
   (d) Relative profitability of food and non-food crops.

110. Marketing of agriculture produce is characterised by certain features which necessitate special arrangements for it's sale. Among these the more important are.

   (a) Collection of agriculture produce poses a problem as it is scattered over a vast geographical areas .
   (b) Large difference in qualities and varieties
   (c) Perishable nature of agricultural products
   (d) Seasonal nature of output.

111. One of the following is not a hurdle in the way of ceiling on holding. Which?

   (a) The time gap between the announcement of the policy and enactment of laws on the one hand, and implementation on the other has enabled owners to indulge in all sort of fictitious transfer to get over the provisions of ceiling laws
   (b) Defective conception of the law providing numerous exemption.
   (c) Non-existence of records and lack of honest, efficient administrative machinery
   (d) Political necessity to push through the ceiling on holidays.

112. One of the following is not a solution for the problem of sub-divison and fragment action of holding

(a) Consolidation of holding
(b) Ceiling on holding
(c) Cooperative farming
(d) Restriction and modification in the law of inheritance.

113. The various factors that determine crop pattern in India are given below. One of them is a non economic factor, Which?

(a) Price of various agricultural goods
(b) The area of operational holding
(c) The system under which land is owned
(d) Availability of required inputs.

114. Which one of the following is not the objective of agriculture price policy?

(a) To ensure remunerative prices to the farmer
(b) To prevent sharp fluctuations in farmer's income
(c) To ensure sufficient profits to the farmers
(d) To ensure reasonable prices to the consumers.

115. Which one of the following will you classify as an institutional factor responsible for low productivity in Indian agriculture?

(a) Inadequate inputs and primitive techniques
(b) Tradition bound million of the village
(c) Shortage of finance
(d) Small size of holdings.

116. Which of the following is inconsistent with the other

(a) Tenurial reforms
(b) Consolidation of holdings
(c) Abolition of zamindari
(d) Provision of insecticides.

117. In India the value of output originating in the agriculture with the help of the following method.

(a) Net income method
(b) Net income method

(c) Net income and expenditure method

(d) Net output method.

118. Tenancy reforms in India have suffered from a number of defects but not one of the following:

(a) In respect of a large number of laws there to be found many exceptions and escape clauses which have been misused against the interest of the cultivator

(b) Restrictions on ejection of tenants have been largely evaded by landowners

(c) Tenants have not been supplied with adequate inputs and other scarce productive resources

(d) The law concerning tendency reforms have not been fully implemented.

119. Agricultural credit needs are distinct from those of non-agricultural sector in many respects among which one of the following does not appear:

(a) Needs for agricultural credit remain stable

(b) It is difficult to estimate correctly the credit needs in advance as impossible in the case of non-agricultural industries

(c) An agriculturist can pass on the risk of his business to other people through the sale of shares

(d) Only tangible asset that agriculturists can offer as security against loan is land itself.

120. The major sources of direct finance for agriculture are given below. One of them is not which?

(a) Reserve Bank of India

(b) Regional Rural Bank

(c) Punjab National Bank

(d) Central Bank of India.

ANSWERS

1.	(c)	2.	(a)	3.	(a)	4.	(b)
5.	(d)	6.	(a)	7.	(a)	8.	(a)
9.	(b)	10.	(c)	11.	(a)	12	(d)

13.	(b)	14.	(a)	15.	(b)	16.	(a)
17.	(b)	18.	(a)	19.	(b)	20.	(c)
21.	(d)	22.	(a)	23.	(b)	24.	(b)
25.	(a)	26.	(b)	27.	(d)	28.	(a)
29.	(d)	30.	(a)	31.	(c)	32.	(b)
33.	(c)	34.	(a)	35.	(d)	36.	(d)
37.	(c)	38.	(d)	39.	(a)	40.	(c)
41.	(b)	42.	(c)	43.	(b)	44.	(b)
45.	(d)	46.	(b)	47.	(a)	48.	(d)
49.	(d)	50.	(a)	51.	(b)	52.	(a)
53.	(a)	54.	(b)	55.	(a)	56.	(b)
57.	(c)	58.	(b)	59.	(a)	60.	(b)
61.	(c)	62.	(d)	63.	(b)	65.	(a)
65.	(a)	66.	(a)	67.	(c)	68.	(a)
69.	(d)	70.	(a)	71.	(e)	72.	(d)
73.	(e)	74.	(b)	75.	(d)	76.	(c)
77.	(d)	78.	(a)	79.	(a)	80.	(c)
81.	(d)	82.	(b)	83.	(c)	84.	(c)
85.	(c)	86.	(a)	87.	(d)	88.	(d)
89.	(a)	90.	(b)	91.	(b)	92.	(d)
93.	(c)	94.	(c)	95.	(e)	96.	(e)
97.	(d)	98.	(a)	99.	(a)	100.	(d)
101.	(d)	102.	(d)	103.	(a)	104.	(b)
105.	(b)	106.	(b)	107.	(a)	108.	(d)
109.	(d)	110.	(e)	111.	(d)	112.	(b)
113.	(c)	114.	(c)	115.	(d)	116.	(d)
117.	(c)	118.	(c)	119.	(c)	120.	(a)

8
UNEMPLOYMENT IN INDIA

1. The major causes of unemployment in India can be classified as
   (a) Under development
   (b) Defective planning
   (c) Rapid population growth
   (d) All of the above.

2. Removal of unemployment has been considered a centre-piece of strategy in the
   (a) First plan (b) Third plan
   (c) Fith plan (d) Sixth plan.

3. The annual growth rate of employment during the Seventh Plan period was estimated at the percentage of
   (a) 2 (b) 4
   (c) 6 (d) 8.

4. The phenomenon of structural unemployment is
   (a) Temporary (b) Chronic
   (c) Seasonal (d) Cyclial.

5. Total area as yet unreported for land utilisation as a percentage of the total geographical area is about
   (a) 1 per cent (b) 3.5 per cent
   (c) 7.5 per cent (d) 10.5 per cent.

6. The book *Small is Beautiful* has been written by
   (a) Lloyd G. Reynolds (b) Gerald M. Meier
   (c) E.F. Schumalha (d) V. Shanmugasundram.

7. The IRDP which now incorporates most of the other programmes of rural development covers blacks in the country

(a) 3911 (b) 5011
(c) 4335 (d) 6914.

8. Which one the following is not covere under the Minimum Neads Programme?

(a) Rural Water supply
(b) Social forestry
(c) Elementary education
(d) Improvement urban slum.

9. Under the DRI scheme, at least-percentage of the advances should be made of the SC/ST beneficiaries

(a) 50 (b) 40
(c) 30 (d) 25.

10. Most of the disguised unemployed persons in India are found in

(a) Agriculture (b) Industry
(c) Trade (d) Transport.

11. TRYSEM is a programme of

(a) Rural Development (b) Industrial Development
(c) Defence Preparedness (d) Urban Development.

12. The number of people employed in organised sector is between .... in lakh

(a) 255 and 265 (b) 245 and 250
(c) 220 and 235 (d) 150 and 175.

13. The Food for Work Programme has been restricted as

(a) IDLAD (b) IRDP
(c) MIFAZ (d) NREP.

14. The objective sizeable increase in national income and large long expansion of employment opportunities as

(a) Interrelated (b) Independent
(c) Contradictory (d) None of these.

15. The nature of usual state unemployment is
    (a) Seasonal (b) Disguised
    (c) Chronical (d) Fuctional.

16. Which among the following is the largest programme of rural upliftment?
    (a) MREP (b) IRDP
    (c) RLEGP (d) DPAP.

17. Poverty alleviation programme comprise
    (a) IDP (b) TRYSEM
    (c) RLEGP (d) MNP.
    (e). All of these

18. The SFDA has been merged into
    (a) MIFAL (b) IRDP
    (c) IDLAD (d) TRYSEM.

19. Which one of the following has been started to supplement NREP?
    (a) IDLAP (b) MFAL
    (c) DPAP (d) RLEGP.

20. The relative proportion of labour earning in national income in India is
    (a) Above 70% (b) Above 50%
    (c) Above 90% (d) Above 30%.

21. Jawahar Rozgar Yojana for rural employment was started in the year
    (a) 1959 (b) 1969
    (c) 1979 (d) 1989.

22. The government has been stressing the need for eliminating unemployment since the
    (a) First plan
    (b) Second plan
    (c) Third plan
    (d) Fourth plan.

23. The maximum number of workers are employed in which Industry in India?

(a) Sugar (b) Jute
(c) Textiles (d) Electronic goods.

24. Bonded Labour System (Abolition) Act was passed to the year

(a) 1949 (b) 1956
(c) 1966 (d) 1976.

25. During the Seventh Five Year Plan the employment potential, in terms is standard person years, was expected to increase in (million)

(a) 40 (b) 50
(c) 60 (d) 70.

26. Community Development Programme was launched in India on

(a) 26 January, 1950 (b) 2 October, 1952
(c) 14 November, 1964 (d) 1 April, 1966.

27. The Seventh plan aimed at creating to fall additional employment of the order of

(a) 30 million persons years
(b) 44.1 million persons years
(c) 40.0 million persons years
(d) 54.3 million persons years.

28. Under the new scheme of employment generation in the rural area, all the ongoing scheme and have been amalgamated with the

(a) National Rural Employment Programme
(b) Jawahar Rojgar Yojana
(c) Rural Employment Guarantee Programme
(d) Integrated Rural Development Programme.

29. When we argue that small industries generate large volume of employment, what we essentially employ is that.

(a) The number of workers in a small unit will be larger than these in a big unit.

(b) The number of workers employed per unit of capital is large in small units than in a big unit

(c) The number of workers employed to produce consumer goods will be more

(d) All of the above.

30. Disguised unemployment refers to

(a) Persons with no jobs

(b) More persons employed for a job which less can accomplish

(c) Unemployment of many women

(d) Unemployment of people above 60 years in age.

31. Draft five years plan, 1978-83, defines the status unemployment , as consisiting of these workers

(a) Who do not get work throughout the year.

(b) Who did not find even one hour of work during the survey week and are available for work

(c) Who get some work on same days and are looking for work another days ever during the same week.

(d) None of these.

32. The earlier food for work programme has now been converted into.

(a) Intensive area development programme

(b) Integrated rural development programme

(c) Maintain rural employment programme

(d) Minimum needs programme.

33. Open unemployment refers to people

(a) Who are not willing to work

(b) Who are willing but donot get work

(c) Who leave their jobs in search of better ones

(d) Who have been dismissed because of incorrect practices.

34. The realisation or employment objective depends practically in

(a) Increase labour absorption in agriculture and called services

(b) Increase labour intensive techniques in industrial programmes
(c) Paying labourers in term of wage -goods
(d) None of these.

35. Technically, disguised unemployment is defined as a situation in which
(a) The labour is a more important factor as compared to capital.
(b) The contribution of labour, in terms of, cost, is less
(c) The marginal productivity of labour is zero
(d) The marginal productivity of capital is zero.

36. The most important type of unemployment to be met in India is
(a) Functional unemployment
(b) Cyclical unemployment
(c) Disguised unemployment
(d) Structural unemployment.

37. The problem of unemployment in India can be best described as
(a) Cyclical and therfore short term
(b) Seasonal and therefore interest in local conditions
(c) Chronic unemployment
(d) Disguised unemployment

38. Structural unemployment arises due to
(a) Doblahoncy conditions
(b) Heavy industry fias
(c) Surplus of raw materials
(d) Inadequate productive capacity.

39. Once employment is accepted as an object or planned effect
(a) It will effect the pattern of investment
(b) It will be net effect the pattern investment
(c) It wiil require greater investment in programmes with good employment potential
(d) It will mean more emphasis on agriculture.

40. A charge part of employment in the agricultural sector is the type described as
    (a) Structural Unemployment
    (b) Disguised unemployment
    (c) Frictional unemployment
    (d) Cyclical unemployment.

41. What is the main objective of the yo todecy programme?
    (a) Upliftment of urban poor
    (b) Upliftment of Industrial workers
    (c) Upliftment of farmers
    (d) Upliftment of rural poor.

42. The minimum needs programme in India
    (a) Seeks to provide basic socio-economic infrastructure in rural areas for the benefit of the poor
    (b) Seeks to generate a minimum amount or export earnings for the mounting debt service ratio
    (c) Is based on the critical minimum effort theory of economic devolopment
    (d) Provides the hand care of the plan which must be fulfiled at all stages.

43. Which one of the following is not the objective of IRDP
    (a) It seeks to provide avenues of employment to the rural poor
    (b) It seeks to raise the income level of the poor above the poverty line in a lasting basis
    (c) Under it loans and subsidies are given to the identified poor rural families for purchases or income yielding assers
    (d) It seeks to generate employment in heavy industries.

44. The foremost contribution of cooperative movement in India is that it has
    (a) Change the habits and customs of people, fistered economy is spending and curbing wasteful expenditure
    (b) Made available a large blow of credit at lower rate of interest to the people in rural areas

(c) Imparted education to the rural people and make them participate activity in the democratic institutions
(d) Improved farming methods and increased agricultural productivity.

45. Which one of the following is not a part of the strategy of direct attack on poverty,
(a) Integrated Rural Development Programme
(b) Jawahar Rozgar Yojana
(c) National Rural Employment Programme
(d) Family Planning Programme.

46. The commonly development programme covers at present
(a) 50% of rural India
(b) 75% of rural India
(c) 90% of rural India
(d) 100% of rural India.

47. Food for Work Programme was being managed by
(a) The State Bank of India
(b) The I.M.F.
(c) The World Bank
(d) The Reserve Bank of India.

48. The responsibility for policy formula than relating to the community development programme and the broad pattern of expenditure lies with
(a) The development of commonly develoment in the ministry of Agriculture
(b) Development commissioner of the respective states
(c) Agricultural production commissioner
(d) Zila Parishads.

49. Which one the following statements is not correct in the content of the National Rural Employment Programme
(a) It is a centrally sponsored scheme
(b) It aims at creating larger avenues of employment for the rural poor
(c) Under it wages are paid partly in cash and partly in foodgrain

(d) It provides employment opportunities only and schedulod Tribe families.

50. The major sources of direct finance for agriculture are given below one of them it not,which?

(a) Reserve Bank of India

(b) Regional Rural Bank

(c) Punjab National Bank

(d) Central Bank of India.

ANSWERS

1.	(d)	2.	(d)	3.	(b)	4.	(b)
5.	(c)	6.	(c)	7.	(b)	8.	(d)
9.	(b)	10.	(a)	11.	(a)	12.	(a)
13.	(d)	14.	(a)	15.	(c)	16.	(b)
17.	(c)	18.	(b)	19.	(d)	20.	(d)
21.	(d)	22.	(a)	23.	(c)	24.	(d)
25.	(a)	26.	(b)	27.	(c)	28.	(b)
29.	(b)	30.	(b)	31.	(c)	32.	(c)
33.	(d)	34.	(b)	35.	(c)	36.	(c)
37.	(d)	38.	(d)	39.	(c)	40.	(b)
41.	(d)	42.	(d)	43.	(d)	44.	(c)
45.	(d)	46.	(d)	47.	(d)	48.	(d)
49.	(b)	50.	(d)				

9
INDUSTRIAL SCENARIO

1. The focus of 'No industry district scheme' of the government of India is on
   (a) Production increase
   (b) Raw materials supplies
   (c) Employment creation
   (d) Location of industry.
2. Durgapur steel plant was set up with assistance of
   (a) U.K. (b) U.S.A.
   (c) U.S.S.R. (d) West Germany.
3. The strategy of emphasising the rapid growth of heavy and basic industries has an outlook which is
   (a) Short term (b) Long term
   (c) Of immediate benefit (d) None of these.
4. Rapid industrialisation with particular emphasis on the development of basic and heavy industries was one of the objectives of
   (a) First Five Year Plan
   (b) Second Five Year Plan
   (c) Third Five Year Plan
   (d) Fourth five Year Plan.
5. Heavy investment sector comprises of industries with minimum investment of
   (a) Over Rs. 5 crores (b) Over Rs. 7.5 crores
   (c) Over Rs. 10 crores (d) Over Rs. 12.5 crores.

6. The minimum number of persons required to form a primary cooperative society is

(a) 2 (b) 4
(c) 8 (d) 10.

7. The Dutt Committee recommended that

(a) Industrial licenses should be auctioned in future
(b) Industrial licensing system should be altogether dispensed with and replaced by a free market system.
(c) Licensing system should be continued but be modified
(d) Small-scale sector should be included within the licensing system.

8. The Industrial Policy Resolution sought to lay down the framework of a

(a) Mixed economy
(b) Capitalist economy
(c) Laissez- fair type of economy
(d) Balanced growth strategy.

9. Industrial Licensing Policy Inquiry Committee had defined large independent companies as that concerns which had capital assets above

(a) Rs. 5 crores (b) Rs. 25 crores
(c) Rs. 50 crores (d) Rs.100 crores.

10. Largest share of cloth availability in India is contributed by

(a) Mill sector (b) Decentralised sector
(c) Imports (d) Large industries.

11. Among the industrialised nations of the world India ranks among the

(a) Top two (b) Top five
(c) Top eight (d) Top ten.

12. The responsibility of maintaining the supply of essential consumer goods was placed on

(a) Large scale industries
(b) Small scale industries

(c) Consumer co-operative
(d) Traders.

13. The Indian iron and steel industry made its beginning in 1970 with the setting up of the first factory at

(a) Durgapur (b) Bhilai
(c) Jamshedpur (d) Kulti.

14. The origin of the cotton textile industry dates back to 1818 when the first mill was established at

(a) Bombay
(b) Fort Gloste near Calcutta
(c) Madras
(d) Ahmedabad.

15. The first public sector fertilizer factory that went into production in 1951 is located at

(a) Nangal (b) Sindri
(c) Talcher (d) Gorakhpur.

16. Jute industry in India is concentrated at

(a) Assam (b) Kerala
(c) Bangalore (d) Orissa.

17. Tiny sector now includes industrial units with capital investment of less than

(a) Rs. 1 lakh (b) Rs. 5 lakhs
(c) Rs. 7.5 lakh (d) 10 lakh.

18. Medium term finance is usually for a period ranging up to

(a) 1 year (b) 3 years
(c) 5 years (d) 10 years.

19. From May 30, 1990 onwards the limit of fixed capital assets in the small scale industries has been increased from

(a) Rs. 25 to 40 lakhs
(b) Rs. 35 to 60 lakhs
(c) Rs. 45 to 75 lakhs
(d) Rs. 55 to 90 lakhs.

20. Among the major agro-based industries in India, sugar industries ranks

(a) First (b) Second
(c) Third (d) Fourth.

21. An Industrial unit is now categorised into small scale if it has fixed capital investment of less than

(a) Rs. 25 lakh (b) Rs. 35 lakh
(c) Rs. 60 lakh (d) Rs. 75 lakh.

22. Industries in the declared 'backward areas' are exempted from industrial licensing if their investment does not exceed Rs---------------- crores

(a) 100 (b) 50
(c) 25 (d) 15.

23. To which sector is maximum weightage in the index of industrial production assigned?

(a) Managing and quarrying
(b) Manufacturing
(c) Electricity
(d) All equal.

24. A significant feature of the development of sugar industry in India after Independence has been the remarkable expansion of

(a) Co-operative sector
(b) Private sector
(c) Public sector
(d) Corporate sector.

25. Which country assisted India in setting up Bhilai steel plant?

(a) U. S. A. (b) U.K.
(c) U.S.S.R. (d) W. Germany.

26. The most backward state, in terms of industrial value added among the following is

(a) Punjab (b) Karnataka
(c) Andhra Pradesh (d) Tamil Nadu.

27. The Oil and Natural Gas Commission was set up in
    - (a) 1956
    - (b) 1957
    - (c) 1958
    - (d) 1959.

28. Largest number of cotton textile mills in India are in the state of
    - (a) Gujarat
    - (b) West Bengal
    - (c) Maharashtra
    - (d) Tamil Nadu.

29. The guarantee scheme which aims at extending ficancial help to small industries was started in the year
    - (a) 1950
    - (b) 1960
    - (c) 1970
    - (d) 1980.

30. The Industrial Finance Corporation of India was set up in the year
    - (a) 1948
    - (b) 1959
    - (c) 1968
    - (d) 1978.

31. The mining of coal which is the major source of energy in India, was started in 1774 at
    - (a) Chindwara
    - (b) Dhanbad
    - (c) Ranchi
    - (d) Raniganj.

32. Investment-wise the biggest sector enterprise in India is
    - (a) National T. P.C.
    - (b) Coal India Ltd.
    - (c) Steel Authority of India
    - (d) Oil and Natural Gas Commission.

33. The first iron and steel unit known as Tata Iron and Steel Company was established in the year
    - (a) 1877
    - (b) 1977
    - (c) 1907
    - (d) 1927.

34. India's shares in the total world production of crude steel is about
    - (a) 1 per cent
    - (b) 3 per cent
    - (c) 5 per cent
    - (d) 7 per cent.

35. If an industry uses a credit for repair, replacement and maintenance of machines, etc. it will be called

(a) Short term finance (b) Medium term finance

(c) Long-term finance (d) None of the above.

36. In terms of value-added, most industrialised developed state of India is

(a) Maharashtra (b) Tamil Nadu

(c) Andhra Pradesh (d) Karnataka.

37. In which of the following products, 100 per cent output is provided in the public sector

(a) Aluminium (b) Steel

(c) Petroleum (d) Fertilizers.

38. The most important competitor of Indian industry is

(a) China (b) Nepal

(c) Bangla Desh (d) Japan.

39. The production capacity of Bokaro Steel Plant is

(a) 18 lakh in got tonnes

(b) 25 lakh in got tonnes

(c) 16 lakh in got tonnes

(d) 40 lakh in got tonnes.

40. Which of the following steel plants produces stainless stees sheets and coils?

(a) Durgapur steel plant

(b) Visvesvaraya steel works

(c) Salem steel project

(d) Indian iron and steel company.

41. The Small Industries Development Bank of India was set up in the year?

(a) 1960 (b) 1970

(c) 1980 (d) 1990.

42. Cottage and small scale industries are generally

(a) Labour intensive (b) Capital intensive

(c) Labour saving (d). None of the above.

43. The MRP Act defines a large house as one with assets of not less than

(a) Rs. 40 crores (b) Rs. 30 crores
(c) Rs.100 crores (d) Rs. 10 crores.

44. Annual growth rate of industrial production in India has been highest during the period

(a) 1955-60 (b) 1960-65
(c) 1965-70 (d) 1970-75.

45. The annual growth rate of industrial production during the planning era, has, generally, been

(a) More than 10 percent
(b) More than 8 percent
(c) More than 5 percent
(d) More than 2 percent.

46. The village and small industries committee reported in the year

(a) 1955 (b) 1965
(c) 1975 (d) 1980.

47. Which of the following fertilizer plant is not in the public sector

(a) Gorakhpur (b) Kota
(c) Nangal (d) Bhatinda.

48. India Telephone Industries Ltd is located at:

(a) Bombay and Bangalore
(b) Bangalore
(c) Bombay and New Delhi
(d) Bombay and Madras.

49. The need to modernise techniques of production is most imperative in

(a) Cotton textile industry
(b) Jute industry
(c) Sugar industry
(d) All of the above.

50. In the strategy of development adopted the responsibility for the development of heavy capital goods industries was placed largely on

(a) Private sector (b) Public sector
(c) Joint-sector (d) Co-operative sector.

51. In pre-planning period, the most of the industries that had developed were

(a) Metal-based (b) Agro-based
(c) Chemical-based (d) All of the above.

52. At present the Bumber of commodities reserved for exclusive production in the small sector runs to

(a) 108 (b) 504
(c) 653 (d) 836.

53. Manufacture of cement was started in India in 1904 at

(a) Ahmedabad (b) Kota
(c) Madras (d) Trivandrum.

54. The annual production of industrialand fuel wood in India is estimated at

(a) 10 million cubic metres
(b) 20 million cubic metres
(c) 30 million cubic metres
(d) 40 million cubic metres.

55. Rourkela steel plant was set up with assistance from

(a) U.S.S.R. (b) West Germany
(c) U.K. (d) U.S.A.

56. Under schedule B of 1956 industrial policy how many industries were included?

(a) Fifteen (b) Sixteen
(c) Twelve (d) Eleven.

57. The industrial policy announced on May 31,1990 raised the investment limit for small scale sector from Rs. 35 lakhs to Rs.

(a) 45 lakhs (b) 60 lakhs
(c) 75 lakhs (d) 90 lakhs.

58. Oldest large scale industry of India is
(a) Cotton textile industry
(b) Jute industry
(c) Iron and steel industry
(d) Cement industry.

59. The state financial corporotions are prohibited from extending loans to
(a) Small industries
(b) Medium industries
(c) Large industries
(d) None of the above.

60. The cooking coal and non-cooking coal mines were nationalised in
(a) 1971and 1972 respectively
(b) 1972 and 1973 respectively
(c) 1973 and 1970 respectively
(d) 1970 and 1972 respectively.

61. The Industrial Development Bank of India is
(a) A subsidiary of the R.B.I
(b) A department of the R.B.I
(c) An autonomous public sector institution
(d) A private sector Bank.

62. A large share of investment in the public sector is accounted for by
(a) Consumer goodsindustries
(b) Light capital goods industries
(c) Heavy capital goods industries
(d) Defence production.

63. In which of the following sectors is not playing an increasing important rate?
(a) Civil aviation, defence equipment
(b) Heavy capital goods industries
(c) Agriculture
(d) Industries of national importance.

64. The heavy-industry-led growth strategy can be summed up in the phase
    (a) More consumption for future generations
    (b) Less consumption for future generations
    (c) Let the cake grow
    (d) More consumption for present and less capital accumulation.

65. The top profit making enterprise of the government of India is
    (a) Steel Authority of India Ltd.
    (b) Oil and Natural Gas Commission
    (c) Mahanagar Telephone Nigam
    (d) National Thermal Power Corporation.

66. Most of the problems of small industries arise because
    (a) Of the smallness of their size
    (b) These industries are now aware of their needs
    (c) The government has not been voilling to help them
    (d) Of the lack of the political will.

67. Small scale and cattage industries have been assigned an important place in India mainly because of
    (a) The cease of starting and managing them
    (b) The protection they enjoy from the state
    (c) The small capital they need
    (d) The large employment they generate.

68. " Food, work and productivity" was the focus of
    (a) Fifth plan (b) 6th plan
    (c) 4th polan (d) 7 th plan.

69. The seventh plan envisaged an average annual growth rate of
    (a) 15 per cent
    (b) 6 per cent
    (c) 9.5 per cent
    (d) 6.5 per cent.

70. Which of the following is the criterion for demarcating an industry as small, medium or large scale?
   (a) The amount of fixed capital invested
   (b) The number of people employed
   (c) The size of the market
   (d) The value of turn over.

ANSWERS

1.	(d)	2.	(a)	3.	(b)	4.	(b)
5.	(b)	6.	(d)	7.	(c)	8.	(a)
9.	(a)	10.	(b)	11.	(d)	12.	(b)
13.	(d)	14.	(b)	15.	(b)	16.	(c)
17.	(b)	18.	(c)	19.	(b)	20.	(b)
21.	(c)	22.	(b)	23.	(b)	24.	(a)
25.	(a)	26.	(a)	27.	(d)	28.	(c)
29.	(b)	30.	(a)	31.	(d)	32.	(a)
33.	(c)	34.	(a)	35.	(b)	36.	(a)
37.	(c)	38.	(c)	39.	(d)	40.	(c)
41.	(d)	42.	(c)	43.	(b)	44.	(b)
45.	(c)	46.	(a)	47.	(b)	48.	(b)
49.	(d)	50.	(b)	51.	(b)	52.	(d)
53.	(c)	54.	(b)	55.	(b)	56.	(c)
57.	(b)	58.	(a)	59.	(c)	60.	(b)
61.	(c)	62.	(c)	63.	(c)	64.	(c)
65.	(b)	66.	(a)	67.	(d)	68.	(d)
69.	(a)	70.	(a)				

SET 1
ASSESS YOURSELF

1. Which of the following cannot be described as an achievement of the public sector for in India
   (a) Over-capitalisation
   (b) Strengthening infrastructure
   (c) Introducing modern technology
   (d) Economies of scale.

2. The prices of products of public sector enterprises should be
   (a) Lower than the costs income
   (b) Highly remunerative
   (c) Able to achieve the social objectives
   (d) None of the above.

3. The All India Khadi and Village Industries Board was set up during the
   (a) First plan (b) Second plan
   (c) Third plan (d) Fourth plan.

4. The Khadi and Village Industries Commission (KVIC) was set up during the
   (a) First plan (b) Second plan
   (c) Third plan (d) Fourth plan.

5. The Indian income tax is
   (a) Direct and proportional
   (b) Direct and Progressive
   (c) Indirect and progressve
   (d) Indirect and Progressive.

6. The Finance Commission is appointed at the expiry of every x years or earlier. The number x is

(a) 3 (b) 5
(c) 7 (d) 9.

7. Who was the chairman of the Eighth Finance Commission

(a) J.M. Shelat (b) Mahavir Tyagi
(c) L.K. Jha (d) Y. B. Chavan.

8. The Eighth Finance Commission has retained the percentage of the states share in income tax at

(a) 55 (b) 65
(c) 75 (d) 85.

9. Funds are transferred from the centre to the states as

(a) Recommendation of the finance commission
(b) Centre's additional assistance and Loans
(c) Assistance from Planning Commission
(d) All of these.

10. The extent of deficit financing during the second plan has been estimated at (Rs crore)

(a) 354 (b) 954
(c) 1,554 (d) 2154.

11. Which of the following is not a central government tax ?

(a) Income tax (b) Customs
(c) Land revenue (d) Corporation tax.

12. Which of the following is a direct tax?

(a) Entertainment tax (b) Estate duty
(c) Excise duty (d) Sales tax.

13. Which of the following is an indirect tax?

(a) Customs (b) Corporation tax
(c) Wealth tax (d) Gift tax.

14. A tax that takes away a higher proportion of one's income as the income rises in terms as a

(a) Progressive tax (b) Proportional tax
(c) Regressive (d) Indirect tax.

15. In a doveloping economy there is a case for
   (a) No taxation
   (b) Regressive taxation
   (c) Progressive taxation
   (d) Professional taxation.

16. Inflation is caused by
   (a) Increase in money supply
   (b) Increase in production
   (c) Decrease in production
   (d) Both (a) and (c).

17. Which of the following is not a cause of inflation?
   (a) Deficit financing
   (b) Rapid population growth
   (c) Increasing non-development expenditure of the government
   (d) Increasing expenditure on fertilisers.

18. Which of the following is not a cause of inflation?
   (a) Slow growth in agricultural output
   (b) Slow growth in industrial output
   (c) Slow growth in population
   (d) Rapid growth in costly imports.

19. Which of the following is not a care for inflation?
   (a) Better capacity utilisation
   (b Lowering of bank rate
   (c) Public distribution system
   (d) Lowering of budget deficit.

20. The extent of deficit financing during the first plan has been estimated at (Rs. crore)
   (a) 333 (b) 666
   (c) 999 (d) 1111.

21. The general price level declined during the
   (a) First plan (b) Second plan
   (c) Third plan (d) Fourth plan.

22. During the second plan, the wholesale price index increased by about

(a) 10 per cent (b) 20 per cent
(c) 30 per cent (d) 40 per cent.

23. During the third plan, the wholesale price index increased by about

(a) 5 per cent (b) 15 per cent
(c) 25 per cent (d) 35 per cent.

24. India suffered from first oil shock in

(a) 1969 (b) 1971
(c) 1973 (d) 1975.

25. India suffered from second oil shock in

(a) 1973 (b) 1975
(c) 1977 (d) 1979.

26. India suffered from third oil shock in

(a) 1983-84 (b) 1990-91
(c) 1985-86 (d) 1987-88.

27. The build up of inflationary pressures in recent years is due to

(a) Fiscal imbalance
(b) Supply and demand
(c) Persistent pressure on balance of payments
(d) All the above.

28. Which of the following is not a poverty removal programme

(a) NREF (b) HYV
(c) IRDP (d) RLEGP.

29. The 'Garibi Hatao' (eradicate poverty) slogan was coined during the

(a) First plan (b) Second plan
(c) Third plan (d) Fourth plan.

30. The Minimum Needs Programme was initiated during the

(a) First plan (b) Second plan
(c) Third plan (d) Fourth plan.

31. During the first plan, the wholesale price index declined by about
(a) 12 per cent (b) 2 per cent
(c) 22 per cent (d) 32 per cent.

32. The price rise in India has been a continuous phenomenon since
(a) First plan (b) Second plan
(c) Third plan (d) Fourth plan.

33. SIDO is related to the development of
(a) Small industries (b) Steel industry
(c) Soap industry (d) Sugar industry.

34. The most important small-scale industry in India is the
(a) Textile industry
(b) Paper industry
(c) Handloom industry
(d) Jute industry.

35. The major source of finance for small scale industries is
(a) Shares and debentures
(b) Bank loan
(c) Public deposits
(d) Foreign aid.

36. ICICI is the name of a
(a) Financial institution
(b) Chemical industry
(c) Cotton industry
(d) Chamber of Commerce and industry.

37. IDBI is a
(a) Bank (b) Board
(c) Bureau (d) Corporation.

38. The new name of IRCI is
(a) IDBI (b) IRBI
(c) ICICI (d) IFCI.

39. IFCI is the name of a
    (a) Fertiliser company
    (b) Federation of Commerce and Industry
    (c) Financial institution
    (d) None of these.

40. Which of the following taxes is not shared by the Central Government with the States?
    (a) Union excise duties (b) Customs duty
    (c) Income tax (d) Estate duty.

41. Fiscal policy is connected with
    (a) Exports and imports
    (b) Public revenue and expenditure
    (c) Issue of currency
    (d) Population control.

42. The most important source of public revenue is
    (a) Taxes (b) Interest
    (c) Dividends and profits (d) Licence fees.

43. Which of the following is the largest single source of the governments earning from tax revenue?
    (a) Excise (b) Customs
    (c) Corporation tax (d) Income tax.

44. Out of the following which one contributes the minimum amount to the governments tax revenue?
    (a) Excise (b) Customs
    (c) Wealth tax (d) Income tax.

45. Which of the following is the major source of government revenue
    (a) Direct taxes (b) Indirect taxes
    (c) Interest (d) Dividends and profits.

46. The safe of land reforms does not include
    (a) Abolition of intermediaries
    (b) Consideration of land holdings

(c) Cooperative farming
(d) Housing loans to farmers.

47. Successful implementation of land reforms ensures
(a) Growth with justice
(b) Growth without justice
(c) Justice without growth
(d) Neither growth nor Justice.

48. Land reform policies in India have met with
(a) Tremendous success (b) Complete failure
(c) Limited success (d) None of these.

49. Indian agriculture there is a need for
(a) Rapid mechanisation
(b) No mechanisation
(c) Selective and restricted mechanisation
(d) None of these.

50. The land ceiling legislation was actually introduced by the State Governments during the
(a) First plan (b) Second plan
(c) Third plan (d) Fourth plan.

ANSWERS

1.	(a)	2.	(c)	3.	(a)	4.	(b)
5.	(c)	6.	(b)	7.	(d)	8.	(d)
9.	(d)	10.	(b)	11.	(c)	12.	(b)
13.	(a)	14.	(a)	15.	(c)	16.	(d)
17.	(d)	18.	(c)	19.	(b)	20.	(a)
21.	(a)	22.	(c)	23.	(d)	24.	(c)
25.	(d)	26.	(b)	27.	(d)	28.	(b)
29.	(d)	30.	(d)	31.	(c)	32.	(b)
33.	(a)	34.	(a)	35.	(b)	36.	(a)
37.	(a)	38.	(b)	39.	(c)	40.	(b)
41.	(b)	42.	(a)	43.	(c)	44.	(c)
45.	(b)	46.	(d)	47.	(a)	48.	(c)
49.	(c)	50.	(b)				

SET 2
ASSESS YOURSELF

1. Indian economy is most appropriately described as a
   (a) Capitalist economy
   (b) Mixed economy
   (c) Socialist economy
   (d) None of these.

2. The term mixed economy implies the coexistence of
   (a) Large-scale and small scale industries
   (b) Domestic industry along with multinational
   (c) Agriculture and Industry
   (d) Private and public sector.

3. Who wrote a book describing the theory of economic drain of India during British rule?
   (a) Dadabhai Noaroji (b) Lala Lajpat Rai
   (c) Mahatma Gandhi (d) Jawaharlal Nehru.

4. In recent years the Indian economy has been characterised as a
   (a) Backward economy (b) Developed economy
   (c) Developing economy (d) None of these.

5. Attachment to land, the joints family system and the caste system have retarded Indian economic development. These are
   (a) Political factors (b) Social factors
   (c) Economic factors (d) None of these.

6. Acutal shortage of capital, technological backwardness and lack of skilled man-power have greatly obstructed the economic development of India. These are

(a) Political factor (b) Economic factor
(c) Social factor (d) None of these.

7. Market imperfections in underdeveloped countries are reflected in

(a) Factor immobility (b) Price rigidity
(c) Lack of specialisation (d) All of these.

8. Which of the following does not contribute to the development of the Indian economy?

(a) Population growth (b) Rising industrial
(c) Modern technology (d) Green Revolution.

9. Where does India rank in the world with regard to the size of its population

(a) First place (b) Second place
(c) Third place (d) Fourth place.

10. What is the percentage of India's population to the world population?

(a) 6 per cent (b) 16 per cent
(c) 26 per cent (d) 96 per cent.

11. Which year is known as 'year of the great divide' with regard to Population Growth in India

(a) 1921 (b) 1947
(c) 1951 (d) None of these.

12. The birth rate measure the number of briths during a year per

(a) 100 of population (b) 1000 of population
(c) Million of population (d) None of these.

13. Birth rate in India is high because of the

(a) Joint family system
(b) Social orthodoxy
(c) Desire for a male child
(d) All of these.

14. The only state in India having a sex ratio of above 1000 is
    (a) Tamil Nadu (b) Kerala
    (c) Karnataka (d) Andhra Pradesh.

15. The sex ratio is the lowest in
    (a) Haryana (b) Arunachal Pradesh
    (c) Punjab (d) Nagaland.

16. Which of the following states has a literacy rate of above 90%
    (a) Mizoram (b) Tamil Nadu
    (c) Himachal Pradesh (d) Kerala.

17. Which of the following states has the least literacy rate
    (a) Rajasthan (b) Himachal pradesh
    (c) Uttar Pradesh (d) Madhya pradesh.

18. The maximum number of people in India work in the
    (a) Primary sector (b). Secondary sector
    (c) Tertiary sector (d) All of these.

19. The Reserve Bank of India (RBI) was established in
    (a) 1935 (b) 1947
    (c) 1949 (d) 1951.

20. The RBI was nationalised in
    (a) 1935 (b) 1947
    (c) 1949 (d) 1951.

21. The central banking functions in India are performed by the
    (a) Central Bank of India
    (b) Indian Overseas Bank
    (c) State Bank of India
    (d) Reserve Bank of India.

1. Which of the following is not function of the RBI?
    (a) Bank of ISSUE
    (b) Custodian of forign exchange
    (c) Banker's bank
    (d) Banker to public.

22. The RBI has helped to finance India's foreign trades through

(a) NABARD (b) EXIM bank
(c) State Bank of India (d) IDBI.

23. The RBI has helped to finance India's foreign trades through

(a) NABARD (b) EXIM bank
(c) State Bank of India (d) IDBI.

24. The RBI has been following the policy of

(a) Controlled monetary expansion
(b) Controlled monetary contraction
(c) Unrestricted monetary expansion
(d) Unrestricted monetary contraction.

25. The RBI method of credit control may be broadly divided into two parts

(a) Quantitative and qualitative
(b) Open and close
(c) Monetary and fiscal
(d) Rural and urban.

26. Which of the following is a selective credit control method?

(a) Bank rate
(b) RBI directives
(c) Cash reserves ratio
(d) Open market operation.

27. Bank rate is the rate at which the RBI extends credit to the

(a) Public (b) Foreign countries
(c) Commercial banks (d) Agriculture.

28. Current bank rate in India is

(a) 7 per cent (b) 9 per cent
(c) 12 per cent (d) 15 per cent.

29. Current cash reserve ratio for commerical banks is

(a) 20 per cent (b) 15 per cent
(c) 10 per cent (d) 5 per cent.

30. The statutory liquidity ratio for the commercial banks is
    (a) 8.5 per cent (b) 28.5 per cent
    (c) 18.5 per cent (d) 38.5 per cent.

31. The open market operations refer to the sale and purchase by the RBI of
    (a) Gold (b) Foreign exchange
    (c) Iron and steel (d) Government securities.

32. The *Reserve Bank of India Bulletin* is published every
    (a) Fortnight (b) Month
    (c) Six month (d) Year.

33. The Report on currency and finance is published every
    (a) Fortnight (b) Month
    (c) Six month (d) Year.

34. Which of the following is not an indigenous bank?
    (a) Sarafs
    (b) Chettis
    (c) Land Development Bank
    (d) Mahajans.

35. Indigenous banks are under the direct control of the
    (a) State Bank of India
    (b) Reserve Bank of India
    (c) Regional Rural Bank of India
    (d) None of these.

36. Under the lead Bank scheme a bank was expected to adopt a
    (a) Village (b) Town
    (c) District (d) State.

37. How many subsidiaries does the State Bank of India have
    (a) 3 (b) 5
    (c) 7 (d) 9.

38. India's foreign trade is the highest with
    (a) OECD countries (b) OPEC contries
    (c) East Europen countries (d) Developing countries.

39. The value of the export of merchandise during 1990-91 has been established

(a) 32553 (b) 42553
(c) 52553 (d) 55416.

40. As June 30, 1991 has the approximate population per bank office was

(a) 8000 (b) 14000
(c) 20,000 (d) 26,000.

41. As June 30, 1991 the total number of bank office in India was

(a) 50.190 (b) 60,190
(c) 70,190 (d) 80,190.

42. The value of imports of merchandise during 1990-91 has been established at

(a) 23,193 (b) 33,193
(c) 43,193 (d). 53,193.

43. Since 1951, the importance of UK as India's trading partner has

(a) Remained the same
(b) Gone up
(c) Gone down
(d) UK has creased to be India trading partner.

44. The value of Indian exports to the USA during 1990-91 was

(a) 2797 (b) 3797
(c) 4797 (d) 5797.

45. The Reserve Bank of India (RBI) was established in

(a) 1935 (b) 1947
(c) 1949 (d) 1951.

46. Which of the following can not be described as an achievement of the public sector in India

(a) Over-capitalisation
(b) Strengthening infrastructure
(c) Introducing modern technology
(d) Economics of scale.

47. The prices of products of public sector enterprises should be
    - (a) Lower than the costs incurred
    - (b) Highly remunerative
    - (c) Able to achieve the social object
    - (d) None of these.

48. The All India Khadi and Village Industries Board was set up during the
    - (a) First plan (b) Second plan
    - (c) Third plan (d) Fourth plan.

49. SIDO is related to the development of
    - (a) Small industries (b) Steel industries
    - (c) Soap industry (d) Sugar industry.

50. The RBI was nationalized in
    - (a) 1935 (b) 1947
    - (c) 1949 (d) 1951.

ANSWERS

1.	(b)	2.	(d)	3.	(a)	4.	(c)
5.	(b)	6.	(b)	7.	(c)	8.	(a)
9.	(b)	10.	(b)	11.	(a)	12.	(b)
13.	(d)	14.	(b)	15.	(b)	16.	(d)
17.	(d)	18.	(a)	19.	(a)	20.	(c)
21.	(d)	22.	(d)	23.	(b)	24.	(a)
25.	(a)	26.	(b)	27.	(c)	28.	(c)
29.	(b)	30.	(d)	31.	(d)	32.	(b)
33.	(d)	34.	(c)	35.	(d)	36.	(b)
37.	(c)	38.	(c)	39.	(a)	40.	(c)
41.	(b)	42.	(a)	43.	(d)	44.	(a)
45.	(a)	46.	(a)	47.	(c)	48.	(a)
49.	(a)	50.	(c)				

SET 3
ASSESS YOURSELF

1. The success of the fourth plan was obstructed by
   (a) Poor monsoons
   (b) Problem of Bangladesh refugees
   (c) War with Pakistan
   (d) All of these.

2. The strategic aim of the fifth plan was
   (a) Removal of poverty and attainment of economic self-reliance
   (b) Adult education
   (c) Improving transportation network
   (d) Modernisation of agriculture.

3. The third plan turned out to be
   (a) Moderately successful (b) Highly successful
   (c) Successful (d) A failure.

4. The percentage of the plan development outlay allocated at agriculture and allied sectors in the third plan was approximately
   (a) 12 (b) 13
   (c) 14 (d) 15.

5. Which of the following factors led to the failure of the third plan
   (i) Chinese aggression
   (ii) Indo-aggression

(iii) Devaluation of rupee
(iv) Poor monsoons
(a) (i) and (iii) only
(b) (iii) and (iv) only
(c) (i),(ii) and (iv) only
(d) (i) , (ii), (iii), and (iv).

6. The fourth plan airned at
(a) Balanced regional development
(b) Growth with justice
(c) Progressive achievement of self-reliance
(d) All of these.

7. The sixth plan aimed at strengthening the infrastructure for
(a) Industry (b) Agriculture
(c) Both of these (d) None of these.

8. As compared to the target, the economy during the period 1980-85 has grown at a
(a) Much faster rate
(b) Much slower rate
(c) Rate equal to the target rate
(d) None of these.

9. The correct duration of the seventh five year plan is
(a) 1981-86 (b) 1986-91
(c) 1984-89 (d) 1985-90.

10. The long-term development strategy of the seventh plan gave the highest priority
(a) Heavy and basic industry
(b) Creation of more employment opportunities
(c) Small- scale industry
(d) None of these.

11. The core slogan of the seventh plan was
(a) Food, work and productivity
(b) Community development programmes
(c) Free education for all children
(d) Five per cent growth rate of national income.

12. The maximum weightage in the sectoral allocations of plan development outlay in the seventh plan was given to
    (a) Industry and minerals
    (b) Science and technology
    (c) Energy
    (d) Agriculture and rural development.

13. The first three years of the seventh plan were end of
    (a) Poor monsoons (b) Good monsoons
    (c) Average monsoons (d) Nothing may be said.

14. Which of the following is not problem in the estimation of India's national income
    (a) Non-monetised consumption
    (b) Rapid industrial is a plan
    (c) Illiterate people
    (d) People holding multiple jobs.

15. The difference between the G.N.P and N.N.P is equal to the
    (a) Direct tax revenue
    (b) Indirect tax revenue
    (c) Capital depreciation
    (d) Consumer expenditure on durable goods.

16. Which of the following has not been a feature of the seventh plan during its first three years?
    (a) High surpluses of public sector enterprises
    (b) Weak agricultural performance
    (c) Slow growth is non-plan expenditure
    (d) Pressure on balance of payments.

17. The balance of payments continued to be under pressure during the seventh plan because of
    (a) Protectionist tendencies abroad
    (b) Deceleration in growth of domestic oil production
    (c) Unstability of major international currencies
    (d) All of these.

18. The national income of the a nation is the
    (a) Government's annual revenue
    (b) Exports minus imports
    (c) Surplus of public sector undertakings
    (d) Sum total of factor incomes.

19. The national income in India is estimated by the
    (a) Central Statistical Organisation
    (b) Indian Statistical Institute
    (c) Indian Standards Institution
    (d) National Council for Applied economic Research.

20. Which of the following features of Indian economy cause problems in the measurement of national income
    (i) Illiteracy
    (ii) Rapid growth of public sector
    (iii) Non-monetised consumption in the villages
    (iv) People holding multiple jobs
    (a) (i) and (iii)
    (b) (i) (iii) and (iv)
    (c) (i) (ii) and (iii)
    (d) (ii) (iii) (iv).

21. The largest rice-producing state in India is
    (a) Kerala (b) Bihar
    (c) West Bengal (d) Uttar Pradesh.

22. The Agricultural Prices Commission was set up in
    (a) 1965 (b) 1966
    (c) 1967 (d) 1968.

23. NAFED is connected with
    (a) Agricultural marking
    (b) Animal husbandry
    (c) Conservation of fuels
    (d) Agricultural developments.

24. The main impact of the green revolution has been on
    (a) Pulses (b) Vegetables
    (c) Fruits (d) Cereals.

25. The Green Revolution has led to
    (a) Maximum benefit to the wheat crop
    (b) Increase in inter-personal inequalities
    (c) Increase in regional inequalities
    (d) All these these.

26. The policy of family planning was adopted by the government in-
    (a) 1962 (b) 1952
    (c) 1947 (d) 1956.

27. Most of the disguised unemployed persons in India are found in-
    (a) Transport (b) Trade
    (c) Industry (d) Agriculture.

28. Structural unemployment arises due to
    (a) Heavy industry basis
    (b) Inadequate productive capacity
    (c) Deflationary conditions
    (d) Shortage of raw materials.

29. Disguised unemployment refers to-
    (a) More persons empolyed for a job which a few can accomplish
    (b) Employment of people above 60 years of age
    (c) Persons with no jobs
    (d) Unemployment among weomen.

30. The phenomenon of structural unemployment is-
    (a) Chronic (b) Cyclical
    (c) Temporary (d) Seasonal.

31. Seasonal unemployment refers mainly to
    (a) Banks (b) Agriculture
    (c) Public sector industry (d) Private sector industry.

32. Open unemployment refers to
    (a) Daily status (b) Usual status
    (c) Weekly status (d) None of these.

33. The government has been stressing the need for eliminating unemployment since the

(a) First plan (b) Fourth plan
(c) Second plan (d) Third pplan.

34. The nature of usual status unemployment is-

(a) Frictional (b) Disguised
(c) Seasonal (d) Chronic.

35. Food for Work Programme was introduced during the-

(a) Forth plan
(b) Fifth plan
(c) Sixth plan
(d) Seventh plan.

36. The SFDA has been merged into-

(a) IRDP (b) TRYSEM
(c) MFAL (d) IDLAD.

37. The Food for Work Programme has been restructured as-

(a) IRDP (b) NREP
(c) IDLAD (d) MFAL.

38. The seventh plan gave the highest priority to-

(a) Import substitution
(b) Provision of productive employment
(c) Adult education
(d) Strengthening of transport network.

39. Which of the following has been started to supplement NREP?

(a) DPAP (b) IDLAD
(c) RLEGP (d) MFAL.

40. The ex-officio chairman of the Planning Commission of India is the

(a) Prime minister
(b) Planning minister
(c) Governer of Reserve Bank of India
(d) Finance minister.

41. The Planning Commission of India is
    (a) An advisory body
    (b) A constitutional body
    (c) A statutory body
    (d) An independent and autonomous body.

42. Jawahar Lal Nehru's main emphasis in planning was on development of
    (a) Small scale industries
    (b) Basic and heavy industries
    (c) Trade and commerce
    (d) Employment generation.

43. The overall aim of economic planning in India is-
    (a) Growth with justice
    (b) To generate rural employment
    (c) To increase national income
    (d) To increase industrial output.

44. Which one of the following is not a feature of India's economic planning?
    (a) Indicative planning (b) Imperative planning
    (c) Limited centralisation (d) Democratic socialism.

45. What is the corroct duration of the first plan?
    (a) 1951-56 (b) 1947-52
    (c) 1950-53 (d) None of these.

46. The major emphasis in the first plan was on-
    (a) Employment generation
    (b) Agriculture
    (c) Export promotion
    (d) Industry.

47. Which one of the following is not an objective of India's economic planning?
    (a) Self-reliance
    (b) Population growth
    (c) Employment generation
    (d) Industrial growth.

48. Which of the following was not a major fealure of thefirst plan?
    (a) Community development projects
    (b) Priority to agriculture
    (c) Priority to heavy industries
    (d) Rehabilitation of the economy.

49. What is the correct duration of the third plan?
    (a) 1958-62 (b) 1960-65
    (c) 1959-62 (d) 1961-66.

50. The major emphasis in the third plan was on-
    (a) Food for Work Programme
    (b) Green Revolution
    (c) Adult education
    (d) Making India self reliant.

ANSWERS

1.	(d)	2.	(a)	3.	(a)	4.	(b)
5.	(c)	6.	(d)	7.	(c)	8.	(d)
9.	(d)	10.	(b)	11.	(a)	12.	(c)
13.	(a)	14.	(b)	15.	(c)	16.	(a)
17.	(d)	18.	(d)	19.	(a)	20.	(b)
21.	(c)	22.	(a)	23.	(a)	24.	(c)
25.	(d)	26.	(b)	27.	(d)	28.	(b)
29.	(a)	30.	(a)	31.	(b)	32.	(b)
33.	(a)	34.	(d)	35.	(b)	36.	(a)
37.	(b)	38.	(b)	39.	(c)	40.	(b)
41.	(a)	42.	(b)	43.	(a)	44.	(b)
45.	(a)	46.	(b)	47.	(b)	48.	(c)
49.	(d)	50.	(d)				

SET 4
ASSESS YOURSELF

1. The ratio of exchange between two goods indifference curve analysis is shown by
   (a) The price consumption curve
   (b) The income consumption curve
   (c) The budget line
   (d) The indifference curve.

2. Which of the following statements is correct? Each point on an indifference curve shows:
   (a) Different combinations of two commodities
   (b) Utilities of different combinations of the same commodity
   (c) Utilities of combinations of different commodities
   (d) Different combinations of the same commodity.

3. The slope of the indifference curve shows:
   (a) The price ratio
   (b) Diminishing marginal rate of substitution
   (c) Factor substitution
   (d) Levels of indifference.

4. The indifference curve which is 'L' shaped represents
   (a) Perfect complimentary
   (b) Perfect substitutability
   (c) No substitutability
   (d) Non complementary.

5. The statement C=D=10 utitity implies
   (a) An ordinay measure of utility only
   (b) A cardinal measure of utility only
   (c) An ordinal and cardinal measure of utility
   (d) More of the above.

6. A "budget line" shows
   (a) Price of commodity X in term of Y
   (b) Price of commodity Y in term of X
   (c) Income of the consumer
   (d) All of the above.

7. Indifference curve is downward sloping from left to right since more X and less Y give
   (a) Less satisfaction
   (b) More satisfaction
   (c) Equal satisfaction
   (d) Maximum satisfaction.

8. An indifference curve is usually drawn over to the origin of a graph is illustrated
   (a) Principle of equimarginal utility
   (b) Diminishing marginal technical substitution
   (c) Diminishing marginal technical substitution
   (d) Diminishing marginal utility.

9. MRS xy and MRS xy both will be zero where the commodity x and y are
   (a) Complement to each other
   (b) Substitutes to each other
   (c) Perfect complementarity
   (d) Imperfect complementarity.

10. Which of the following is not a property of indifference curves?
   (a) Convex to the origin
   (b) Slope downwards to the right
   (c) Parallel to each other
   (d) Cannot intersect each other.

11. Diminishing marginal rate of substitution is indicated by
    (a) Convexity of indifference curve
    (b) Downward movement of the indifference curve
    (c) Non intersecting nature
    (d) The slope of indifference curve.

12. The indifference curve approach is based on
    (a) Constant marginal utility of money
    (b) Cardinal measurability of utility
    (c) Diminishing marginal rate of substitution
    (d) None of the above.

13. The slope of the price line throughout its length
    (a) Differs from point to point
    (b) Is the same
    (c) Is equal on other side of the midpoint
    (d) None of the above.

14. The tagency between price line and indifference curve shows
    (a) MRS= p.
    (b) Marginal rate of substitution equals income
    (c) MRSxy -px/py
    (d) MRs- px/py.

15. For perfect complementary between x and y
    (a) MRS xy will be Zero
    (b) MRS yx will be zero
    (c) MRS xy and MRS yx both will be zero
    (d) None of the above.

16. All points on a budget (price) line represent
    (a) Increasing total expenditure
    (b) Decreasing total expenditure
    (c) The same total expenditure
    (d) None of the above.

17. If indifference curve has a positive slope, it means
    (a) Consumer preferences unpredictafic
    (b) Consumer preferences are irrational
    (c) X-is a discommodity
    (d) Y-is a discommodity.

18. For perfect substitutability between x and y:
    (a) MRS xy will be constant
    (b) MRS xy will be decreasing
    (c) MRS xy will be increasing
    (d) None of the above.

19. A movement along given indifference curve is known as
    (a) Income effect (b) Price effect
    (c) Substitution effect (d) None of these.

20. Among the items of durable-use consumer goods, one may find
    (1) ICE cream (2) Pair of shoes
    (3) Loaf of bread (4) Table Fan
    (a) i and 2 only (b) 1and 3 only
    (c) 2 and 4 only (d) 3 and 4 only.
    (e) All of the above

21. If indifference curves are negatively sloped straight lines, then the two goods are
    (a) Perfect complements (b) Perfect substitutes
    (c) Unrelated (d) Normal goods.

22. A consumer is in equilibrium at the point of tangency on his indifference curve and the price line because
    (a) The cannot go below (b) The cannot go beyond
    (c) The cannot go along (d) None of the above.

23. Indifference curve is downward sloping from left to right since more x and less y give
    (a) Less satisfaction
    (b) More satisfaction
    (c) Maximum satisfaction
    (d) Some level of satisfaction.

24. The fact that each want is satiable gives rise to
    (a) The law of substitution
    (b) The law of diminishing marginal utility
    (c) Thek indifference curve analysis
    (d) The revealed preference theory.

25. The amount a consumer is willing to give up to obtain one additional unit of y and still remain on the same indifference curve is measured by
    (a) MRT sxy (b) MRSxy
    (c) MUxy (d) MRS.

26. With the help of diminishing marginal utility and indifference curve, we reach at
    (a) Different conclusions
    (b) Contradiction conclusions
    (c) Similar conclusions
    (d) None of the above.

27. Indifference curves never intersect each other due to
    (a) Different levels of satisfaction
    (b) Same levels of satisfaction
    (c) Convex to origin
    (d) Concave to origin.

28. The Engel Curve passes through the tangency point of
    (a) Budget line and indifference curve
    (b) Price line and isocost line
    (c) Iso-quant and budget line
    (d) None of these.

29. The doctrine of consumer's surplus is based on
    (a) Indifference curve analysis
    (b) Revealed preference theory
    (c) Law of substitution
    (d) The law of diminishing marginal utility.

30. The revealed preference theory was formulated by
    (a) Lionel Robbins (b) Paul Samuelson
    (c) Joan Rabinson (d) Afred Marshall.

31. Consumer's surplus is also known as:

(a) Elasticity of demand (b) Differential surplus
(c) Buyer's surplus (d) Indifference surplus.

32. Consumer's surplus is the highest in the case of

(a) Necessities
(b) Comforts
(c) Luxuries
(d) Conventional necessities.

33. The concept consumer surplus is based on

(a) Law of diminishing marginal utility
(b) Law of equimarginal utility
(c) Law of substitution
(d) Natural law.
(e) None of these

34. An example of commodity having consumer's surplus is:

(a) Salt (b) Costly textile
(c) Machinery (d) Pen.
(e) Foodgrains

35. Consumer's surplus is equal to

(a) Expected utility minus actual utility
(b) Expected utility minus base of utility
(c) Expected utility minus gain of utility
(d) Expected utility plus actual utility.

36. Say in which of the following fields the concert of consumers surplus is useful:

(a) Monetary policy
(b) Tax policy
(c) Investment policy
(d) Fixing remuneration of factors.

37. Consumers surplus is described as:

(a) Extra quantity bought
(b) Low price available

(c) Happiness of the consumer
(d) Difference between actual price and potentials price.

38. While analysing Marshall's measure of consumer surplus one assumes
   (a) Imperfect competition
   (b) Perfect competition
   (c) Monopoly
   (d) Monopoly.

39. The revealed preference theory assumes
   (a) Strong ordering (b) Weak ordering
   (c) Introspection (d) None of these.

40. Slutsky 's theory is consumvtion theory relates to
   (a) Income effect
   (b) Substitution
   (c) Complementary of goods
   (d) Both (a) and (b).

41. An income effect occurs when which of the following takes place?
   (a) An increase in demand is met with an increase in supply
   (b) Price and demand also rise
   (c) A source of supply is limited artificially
   (d) A single price rises or falls relative to other prices.

42. If no special assumption is made, Hicks' compensating variation will be Marshall's consumer surplus
   (a) Less than (b) Greater than
   (c) Equal to (d) Greater or less than.

43. Which of the following shapes illustrates the property of diminishing marginal rate of substitution
   (a) A downward sloping curve convex to origin
   (b) A downward sloping curve convex to origin
   (c) A downward straight line
   (d) An exponential curve.

44. A consumers demand curve can be obtained from
    (a) Income consumption curve
    (b) Engel's curve
    (c) Lorenz curve
    (d) Price consumption curve.

45. For perfect substituatability between x and y
    (a) MRSxy will be increasing
    (b) MRSxy will be decreasing
    (c) MRSxy will be constant
    (d) None of these.

46. The doctrine of consumer surplus is based on
    (a) Revealed preference theory
    (b) Indifference curve analysis
    (c) Law of substitution
    (d) The law of diminishing marginal utility.

47. The price consumption curve for a straight line demand curve extended to both axis:
    (a) Falls throughout
    (b) Rises throughout
    (c) Falls and then rises
    (d) Rises and then falls.

48. The price effect is
    (a) A resultant of the income and substitution effect
    (b) A resultant of the income effect
    (c) A resultant of market conditions and subject evaluation
    (d) None of the above.

49. Who demonstrated the abnormal slope of demand curve for diamonds through the doctrine of conspicuous consumption?
    (a) Throstein Veblen
    (b) Robert Giffen
    (c) David Ricardo
    (d) Alfred Marshall.

50. The Revealed preference theory is based on
    (a) The assumption of indifference
    (b) Utility and demand
    (c) Introspection
    (d) Observed consumer behavior.

ANSWERS

1.	(c)	2.	(a)	3.	(b)	4.	(a)
5.	(c)	6.	(d)	7.	(c)	8.	(b)
9.	(c)	10.	(c)	11.	(d)	12.	(c)
13.	(b)	14.	(c)	15.	(c)	16.	(c)
17.	(c)	18.	(a)	19.	(c)	20.	(c)
21.	(b)	22.	(b)	23.	(d)	24.	(a)
25.	(b)	26.	(c)	27.	(a)	28.	(a)
29.	(d)	30.	(b)	31.	(c)	32.	(a)
33.	(c)	34.	(a)	35.	(b)	36.	(b)
37.	(d)	38.	(b)	39.	(b)	40.	(b)
41.	(d)	42.	(b)	43.	(a)	44.	(c)
45.	(c)	46.	(d)	47.	(b)	48.	(a)
49.	(a)	50.	(d)				

SET 5
ASSESS YOURSELF

1. "Theory of demographic transition" population explosion occurs in the second stage within
   (a) High birth rate meets with high death rate
   (b) Low birth rate meets with low death rate
   (c) Low birth rate meets with high death rate
   (d) High birth rate meets with low death rate.

2. The economist who warned against population explosion is
   (a) Alfred Marshall (b) Karl Marx
   (c) Malthus (d) None of the above.

3. Growth rate of population can be measured as
   (a) Division of death rate by birth rate
   (b) Multiplication of death rate by birth rate
   (c) Addition of death rate and birth rate
   (d) Subtraction of death rate from birth rate.

4. Which of the following refers to the different stages of demographic transition in order?
   (a) Low death rate and high birth rate, low birth rate and low death rate and high birth rate and death rate
   (b) Low death rate and low birth rate, low death rate and high birth rate, high birth rate and death rate
   (c) High death rate and high birth rate, low death rate and high birth rate, low death rate and low birth rate
   (d) None of these.

5. Which is the least densety populated states in India?
   (a) Rajasthan (b) Nagaland
   (c) Gujarat (d) M.P.
6. Accoroding to the census of 1981, India's population during 1971-80 registered, an increase of
   (a) 25.00 per cent (b) 24. 75 per cent
   (c) 23.00 per cent (d) 22.75 per cent.
7. Large Percentage of the population in the age group 0-14 years indicates the presence of
   (a) Unproductive consumers
   (b) Working force
   (c) High death rate
   (d) Low birth rate.
8. The Indian wage policy is most nearly described as being based on
   (a) Productivity (b) Minimum needs
   (c) Standard of living (d) Cost of living.
9. The density of the union territory of Delhi is approximately
   (a) 1200 (b) 2200
   (c) 3200 (d) 4200.
10. The rate of growth of population has been highest during the decade
    (a) 1901-11 (b) 1921-31
    (c) 1951-61 (d) 1961-71.
11. The approximate percentage of population that lives in village is
    (a) 50 (b) 60
    (c) 70 (d) 76.
12. The birth rate measures the numbers of births during a year per
    (a) 100 of population (b) 1000 of population
    (c) Million of population (d) None of the above.

13. Density of population indicates the

(a) Capital-land ratio (b) Land-output ratio
(c) Land-labour ratio (d) Man-land ratio.

14. Life expetancy refers to the number of years a new born child come expect to live in India, life expectancy has been very low as compared to that in other countries, and, over the years, it has

(a) Remained stagment
(b) Shown some increase
(c) Actually come down
(d) Not been possible to measure it.

15. According to seventh plan document,the death rate in 1990 was

(a) 6.4 (b) 10.4
(c) 14.4 (d) 18.4.

16. Infant mortality rate refers to

(a) The number of children dying before reaching the school going age
(b) The number of children dying before reaching 3 years of age
(c) The porportion of children dying within a year of their birth
(d) None of the above.

17. According to the seventh plan document, the birth rate in 1990 was aimed at

(a) 19.1 (b) 29.1
(c) 39.1 (d) 49.1.

18. The highest rate of growth of population for India has been recorded for

(a) The 1941-51 decade (b) The 1951-61 decade
(c) The 1961-71 decade (d) The 1971-81 decade.

19. The total population of scheduled castes and scheduled tribes in India according to 1981 census is nearly percent

(a) 17.5% (b) 20.5%
(c) 23.5% (d) 26.5%.

20. Because of absolute increase in India's rural population, we can say
    (a) India is getting more rural
    (b) India is getting urbanised at a fast speed
    (c) India is getting urbanised at a low rate
    (d) None of the above.

21. The normal reproductive age group among the females in India is between
    (a) 14 to 35 years
    (b) 16 to 40 years
    (c) 14 to 44 years
    (d) 18 to 52 years.

22. Family planning in rural areas of India has met with limited success mainly due to
    (a) Wrong planning
    (b) Non-availability of deveces
    (c) Psychological and social orthodoxy
    (d) Non- availabolity of doctors.

23. Sex ratio refers to the number of females in the population per 1000 male population in India over the years, the sex ratio
    (a) Has changed in the favour of women
    (b) Has gone against women
    (c) Has not changed
    (d) None-of the above.

24. Universal immunisation programme for infants and extant mothers was started in India in
    (a) 1975-76 (b) 1977-78
    (c) 1980-81 (d) 1985-86.

25. The family planning programme was officially launched in India for the first time in
    (a) 1950 (b) 1952
    (c) 1955 (d) 1965.

26. The percentage distribution of the age composition India's population shows the highest population to be in the age group.

(a) 0-14 years (b) 15-60 years
(c) 60 and over (d) 0-5 years.

27. Occupational structure refers to

(a) A number of people living in country
(b) Size of working force in a country
(c) Distribution of working force among the different occupations
(d) The nature of different occupations.

28. What is the approximate density of population in India

(a) 516 (b) 416
(c) 316 (d) 216.

29. The total amount to be spent on the family planning programme during the sixth plan was approximately in Rs.------ crores?

(a) 1,100 (b) 2,200
(c) 4,400 (d) 8,800.

30. Almost all estimates of poverty in India are related to expenditure on food which generates

(a) 1,000 calories per capita per day
(b) 1,650 calories per capita per day
(c) 2,250 calories per capita per day
(d) 2, 750 calories per capita per day.

31. The percentage of population between the poverty line targeted for the terminal year of the seventh plan

(a) 36.8 (b) 25.8
(c) 17.5 (d) 10.8.

32. Dandekar and Rath have estimated the number of people living below the poverty line in 1967 at

(a) 35 percent of population
(b) 41 percent of population

(c) 49% of population
(d) 53% of population.

33. The percentage of the Indian rural population below the poverty line for 1985-85 was

(a) 30.09 (b) 40.62
(c) 45.72 (d) 139.9.

34. One of the following is not a cause of poverty in India-which?

(a) Abundant population
(b) Abundant natural resources
(c) Abundant inaqualities in distribution of income
(d) Abundance of surplus manpower in agriculture.

35. The empirical evidence testifies that as an economy develops, the share of the secondary and tertiary sector in the occupational structure

(a) Falls (b) Rises
(c) Remains unchanged (d) May fall or rise.

36. For international comparisons to measure the level of economic well being in different countries we make use of data relating to

(a) Real national income
(b) Money national income
(c) Real per capita income
(d) Money per capitaincome.

37. Which of the following five years plan had the twin objectives of removal of poverty and attainment of economic self-reliance?

(a) Second (b) Third
(c) Fourth (d) Fifth.

38. The most important remedy to the problem of poverty in India is

(a) Changes in the ownership pattern
(b) Higher productivity
(c) Redistribution of income through fiscal, pricing and other measures

(d) All of the above.

39. For urban areas 'poverty line' has been determined at 1979-80 prices at the income level of
    (a) Rs. 76 per month (b) Rs. 107 per month
    (c) Rs. 122 per month (d) Rs. 98 per month.

40. For rural areas poverty line has been determined at 1984-85 prices at the income level of
    (a) Rs. 76 per month
    (b) Rs. 107 per month
    (c) Rs. 122 per month
    (d) Rs. 96 per month.

41. -------------- by its very nature accentuates inequalities eats into the income of the poor classes and thus leads to deterioration in their economic condition
    (a) Fiscal policy (b) Inflation
    (c) Deflation (d) Monetary policy.

42. According to the seventh plan 1985-90 , the number of people living below the poverty line in rural areas is
    (a) 41 percent (b) 48 percent
    (c) 53 percent (d). 54 percent.

43. The celebrated book '*the Challenge of World Poverty*' has been written by
    (a) Galbraith (b) Kindleberger
    (c) G. Myrdal (d) Dadabhai Noroji.

44. New education policy was anounced by the government of India in
    (a) 1982 (b) 1984
    (c) 1986 (d) 1988.

45. The national policy in education 1986 aims at providing free and compulsory education to all children below the age of 14 years by the year
    (a) 1990 AD (b) 1995 AD
    (c) 2000 AD (d) 2005 AD.

46. Which one of the fallowing union territories has the highest literacy rate?
   (a) Pondicherry (b) Daman and Diu
   (c) Delhi (d) Chandigarh.

47. In urban areas, at 1984-85 prices, the Planning Commission in the seventh plan 1985-90 has defined the poverty line at
   (a) Rs. 65.00 (b) Rs. 122.00
   (c) Rs. 73.50 (d) Rs. 77.20.

48. When a substantial segment of a society is deprived of----- that society is said to plagued with mass poverty
   (a) The minimum necessities
   (b) The minimum livel of living
   (c) Comforts and luxuries
   (d) None of the above.

49. The gross rate of capital formation in India at current prices is ----- percentage of GDP
   (a) 23 to 25 (b) 30 to 33
   (c) 14 to 17 (d) 11 to 14.

50. Per capita income among the following is highest in
   (a) Orissa (b) Assam
   (c) Manipur (d) Kerela.

ANSWERS

1.	(d)	2.	(c)	3.	(d)	4.	(c)
5.	(b)	6.	(a)	7.	(a)	8.	(b)
9.	(d)	10.	(d)	11.	(d)	12.	(b)
13.	(d)	14.	(b)	15.	(b)	16.	(c)
17.	(b)	18.	(d)	19.	(c)	20.	(c)
21.	(c)	22.	(c)	23.	(b)	24.	(d)
25.	(b)	26.	(b)	27.	(c)	28.	(d)
29.	(a)	30.	(c)	31.	(b)	32.	(b)
33.	(d)	34.	(b)	35.	(c)	36.	(c)
37.	(d)	38.	(d)	39.	(c)	40.	(b)
41.	(b)	42.	(a)	43.	(c)	44.	(c)
45.	(b)	46.	(d)	47.	(b)	48.	(b)
49.	(a)	50.	(d)				

SET 6
ASSESS YOURSELF

1. The national income of a nation is
   (a) Government's annual revenue
   (b) Sum total of factor incomes
   (c) Surplus of public sector undertaking
   (d) Exports minus imports.

2. Estimates of national income in India are anually prepared by the
   (a) National income committee
   (b) Central statistical organisation
   (c) Planning Commission
   (d) Reserve Bank of India.

3. In the distribution of India's GDP, the share of which of the following declined between 1960 and 1981?
   (a) Gross domestic development
   (b) Private consumtpion
   (c) Public consumption
   (d) Export of goods and non-factor services.

4. National income calculated at current prices has shown a tendency to rise at a faster rate than national income calculated at constant prices. This is because
   (a) India's population has been rising fast
   (b) Planned expenditure has been increasing fast
   (c) Statistical manupulations are employed by the planners to highlight the achievements

(d) General price level in the economy has been rising fast.

5. The top 20 percent of people in India have a share of about---------- percent in national income

(a) 25 (b) 40
(c) 50 (d) 75.

6. The rate of growth of the NVP at factor cost at 1980-81 prices in the year 1988-87 over 1985-86 has provisionally been estimated as

(a) 1.6% (b) 3.6%
(c) 6.6% (d) 6.5%.

7. Expenditure method is used in calculating the income originating in one of the following sectors. Which is?

(a) Agriculture (b) Mining
(c) Construction (d) Transportation.

8. The GNP at factor cost at the 1970-71 prices for the year 1980-81 was (Rs. crore)

(a) 40,711 (b) 50,711
(c) 60,711 (d) 70,711.

9. The rate of growth of the NNP at factor cost at the 1980-81 prices in the year 1987-88 over 1986-87 has quickly been estimated as--------- percent

(a) 1.4 (b) 3.4
(c) 5.4 (d) 7.4.

10. The NNP of factor cost at the 1970-71 prices for the year 1980-81 was (Rs. crore)

(a) 27,414 (b) 47,414
(c) 37,414 (d) 77,414.

11. The rate of growth of the per capita NNP at factor cost at the 1980-81 prices in the year 1986-87 over 1985-86 has provisionally been estimated as-------- percent

(a) 1.6 (b) 2.6
(c) 5.6 (d) 4.6.

12. The targets of increase in national income were exceeded in performance in India during
    (a) First and second plan
    (b) Second and third plan
    (c) Second and fourth plan
    (d) First and fifth plan.

13. The quick estimate for per capita NNP at the 1980-81 prices for the year 1987-88 is Rs.
    (a) 918 (b) 1,414
    (c) 1,918 (d) 1,418.

14. India's progress has been reasonably satisfactory in connection with
    (a) Reduction of unemployment
    (b) Reduction of inequalities
    (c) Growth of GNP
    (d) Growth of per capita income.

15. The quick estimate of the GNP at factor cost at the 1980-81 prices for the year 1987-88 is
    (a) Rs. 168,919 crore (b) Rs. 189,919 crore
    (c) Rs. 228,919 crore (d) Rs, 259,919 crore.

16. The difference between the GNP and NNP is equal to the
    (a) Consumer expenditure on durable goods
    (b) Direct tax revenue
    (c) Indirect tax revenue
    (d) Capital depreciation.

17. Region-wise, among the following the state at the bottom of the ladder of per capita income is
    (a) U.P (b) J and K
    (c) Punjab (d) Tamil Nadu.

18. The per capita NNP at factor cost at the 1970-71 prices for the year 1980-81 Rs.
    (a) 498 (b) 598
    (c) 698 (d) 798.

19. The GNP at factor cost at the 1980-81 prices for the year 1980-81 was
    (a) Rs. 1,22.571 crore
    (b) Rs. 232,571 crore
    (c) Rs. 422,571 crore
    (d) Rs. 422,771 crore.

20. The lowest minimum per capita income of some African countries according to World-Bank report is
    (a) $ 70 (b) $ 60
    (c) $ 50 (d) $ 55.

21. Personal distribution of national income in India shows
    (a) High degree of enequality
    (b) Low degree of inequality
    (c) Almost complete inequality
    (d) No inequality.

22. The Lorenz-ratio of income distribution in India is between
    (a) 0.37 to 0.39 (b) 0.24 to 0.31
    (c) 0.42 to 0.47 (d) 0.49 to 0.56.

23. According to the World Bank report on Jan. 4,1993 the country top in per capita is
    (a) Kuwait (b) Luxemberg
    (c) Switzerland (d) Japan.

24. India's G.N.P. in 1991, as per World Bank figure was
    (a) $ 243.470 billion (b) $ 245.470 billion
    (c) $ 245.370 billion (d) $ 245.570 billion.

25. India's GNP in 1990 as per World Bank figure was
    (a) $ 242.48 billion (b) $ 246.73 billion
    (c) $ 281.78 billion (d) $ 291.28 billion.

26. Net domestic product of the economy will tend to be more that that the net national product of
    (a) The level of production in private sector of the economy increases

(b) The level of production in both organised and unorganised sectors of the economy increases

(c) The level of production in both organised and unorganised sectors of the economy increases

(d) The net earning from abroad fare negative.

27. Per capita income of India in 1990 was per the debt table was

(a) $ 343 (b) $ 341

(c) $ 326 (d) $ 329.

28. The slow growth rate of per capita income is relative to the growth rate of national income is accounted for by

(a) Slow growth of agricultural sector

(b) Static growth of industrial sector

(c) Rapidly rising prices

(d) Rapid growth of population.

29. What is the approximate percentage share of the secondary sector in India's national income?

(a) 10 (b) 20

(c) 30 (d) 40.

30. The largest share of India's national income originates in the

(a) Primary sector (b) Secondary sector

(c) Tertiary sector (d) Any of the above.

31. Per capita income of India in 1991 as per the debt table was

(a) $ 279 (b) $ 281

(c) $ 283 (d) $ 256.

32. The provisional estimate of the per capita NNP at factor cost at 1980-81 prices for the year 1986-87 is Rs.

(a) 1,892 (b) 2,892

(c) 3,892 (d) 2,732.

33. The difference between national income and domestic product is accounted for by

(a) Export surplus/deficit

(b) Inflow of foreign capital

(c) Net factor income from abroad
(d) Budgetary surplus/deficit.

34. What is the approximate percentage share of the primary sector in India's national income?

(a) 40 (b) 50
(c) 60 (d) 70.

35. The eighth plan will project the incremental capital output ratio of

(a) 4.6 (b) 4.35
(c) 4.20 (d) 4.00.

36. Per capita income of India in 1989 as per the debt table was

(a) $ 323 (b) $ 321
(c) $ 324 (d) $ 326.

37. The rate of growth of gross demestic product envisaged for the sixth plan was

(a) 2.2% (b) 7.2%
(c) 5.2% (d) 6.2%.

38. The 5.0 percent rate of growth implies that

(a) Agricultural production will grow at this rate
(b) Industrial production will grow at this rate
(c) National product will grow at this rate
(d) Per capita product will grow at this rate.

39. The percentage of annual growth rate of NNP at factor cost during the sixth plan was

(a) 3.3 (b) 4.2
(c) 5.3 (d) 6.3.

40. In India GDP is higher than GNP because the country's

(a) Imports are more than exports
(b) Capital inflow is more than capital outflow
(c) Net factor income from abroad is negative
(d) Governments expenditure is more than its income.

ANSWERS

1.	(b)	2.	(b)	3.	(b)	4.	(d)
5.	(c)	6.	(b)	7.	(c)	8.	(b)
9.	(b)	10.	(b)	11.	(a)	12.	(d)
13.	(c)	14.	(c)	15.	(a)	16.	(d)
17.	(a)	18.	(c)	19.	(a)	20.	(a)
21.	(a)	22.	(a)	23.	(c)	24.	(c)
25.	(b)	26.	(a)	27.	(a)	28.	(b)
29.	(b)	30.	(a)	31.	(c)	32.	(a)
33.	(c)	34.	(a)	35.	(b)	36.	(b)
37.	(c)	38.	(c)	39.	(c)	40.	(a)

SET 7
ASSESS YOURSELF

1. The economist who pointed attention of relationship between economic growth and structural changes was
   (a) J.M Keynes (b) Maurice Dobb
   (c) J.R. Hicks (d) Simon Kuznets.

2. As economic growth proceds
   (a) The share of primary sector in national products falls
   (b) The share of secondary sector rises
   (c) The share of tertiary sector rises
   (d) All the above.

3. In India during the process of economic growth during the past four decades
   (a) The share of manufacturing sector in national product has risen at a faster rate than that of tertiary sector
   (b) The share of tertiary sector has almost remained constant
   (c) The share of agricultural sector in national product has registered a decline
   (d) All of the above.

4. India's exports
   (a) Are concentrated only a few primary commodities
   (b) Are concentrated only to a few engineering goods
   (c) Are controlled only a few countries
   (d) None of the above.

5. During eighties, India's import consist mainly of:
   (a) Capital goods and transports equipmint
   (b) Foodgrains and fertiiisers
   (c) Maintenance imports
   (d) Petroleum products.

6. During the past four decades India's population has increased at an annual average rate of:
   (a) 20 percent (b) 2 percent
   (c) 0.2 percent (d) 0 percent.

7. The increase in population recorded during the past four decades has been a consequence of:
   (a) Large-scale migration of population from Nepal and Bangladesh
   (b) A fall in death rate
   (c) A fall in the birth rate
   (d) A fall in death rate and high birth rate.

8. When India enters the third stages of demographic transition
   (a) Its death rate will become zero
   (b) Its births rate will register a significant fall
   (c) Its birth rate will become zero
   (d) Net migration.

9. A dualistic economy is characterised by the existence of:
   (a) Agriculture and industries
   (b) Transport and communication
   (c) Trade and commerce
   (d) None of the above.

10. India is a dualistic economy because?
   (a) Backward techniques of production co-exist along with sophisticated techniques
   (b) Public sector exists along side with private sector
   (c) Both exports and imports of iron and steel
   (d) None of the above.

11. During 1950-92, India's real national income has increased at a slower rate than nominal national incomes
    (a) Because India's population has been rising
    (b) Because price level has been rising
    (c) Because inequalities income distribution have been rising
    (d) None of the above.
12. Per capita income will rise faster than national income
    (a) If the price level remains constant
    (b) If distribution of income remains constant
    (c) If population remains constant
    (d) None of the above.
13. Economic growth is measurable and directly related to:
    (a) 3.5 percent
    (b) Over 2 percent
    (c) 1.5 percent
    (d) Any of the above.
14. In Infrastructure of an economy we include
    (a) Power (b) Transport
    (c) Banking (d) All of the above.
15. In India all infrasturucture
    (a) Is monopoly
    (b) Espartially state monopoly
    (c) Is private owned
    (d) None of the above.
16. Pick up the incorrect statement from the following
    (a) Before independence, foreign capital dominated all capital goods industries
    (b) Before independence, native capital and enterprises were interested only in jute and plantation industries
    (c) Foreign aid was flowing in uncontrolled dimension
    (d) All the above.

17. Laissez faire implies
    (a) Government intervention in all spheres of economic activity
    (b) Government monopoly over all productive activities
    (c) Government monopoly over infrastructure
    (d) None of the above.

18. State participation and intervention in economic activity is a characterstic feature of
    (a) A socialistic economy
    (b) A mixed economy
    (c) A capitalistic economy
    (d) None of the above.

19. When compared to the Indian economy, economic system adopted in the U.S.A. should be described as:
    (a) A capitalistic system
    (b) A mixed capitalistic system
    (c) A democratic socialistic system
    (d) A totally free economy.

20. When compared to the USA, Indian economic system can be described as:
    (a) A capitalistic economy
    (b) A mixed capitalistic economy
    (c) A democratic socialistic economy
    (d) A tatally control system.

21. Democratic socialism implies:
    (a) An all- powerful central outhority
    (b) A democratic political framework
    (c) State ownership over means of production
    (d) All of the above.

22. The first industrial policy resolution was presented in
    (a) 1947 (b) 1948
    (c) 1949 (d) 1950.

23. The IPR 1948 provided for:
    (a) State participation in industry
    (b) Private participation in industry
    (c) Foreign capital participation in industry
    (d) All of the above.

24. Present industrial policy is based on:
    (a) IPR 1948 (b) IPR 1956
    (c) Nip 1991 (d) Nip 1992.

25. Public sector is India is so designed:
    (a) As to supplant private sector
    (b) As to supplement private sector
    (c) As to encourage joint sector
    (d) None of the above.

26. Public enterprises in India have developed only in:
    (a) Key and basic industries
    (b) Consumer's industries
    (c) Service industries
    (d) All types of industries.

27. Reserve Bank of India is the country's:
    (a) Biggest commercial bank
    (b) Central bank
    (c) Biggest cooperative bank
    (d) All of the above.

28. Reserve Bank of India issues all currency in India except:
    (a) One-rupee note
    (b) Two-rupee note
    (c) Five-rupee note
    (d) Ten-rupee note.

29. The largest proportion of national income in India is contributed by private sector. This shows that:
    (a) Public sector is in its infancy
    (b) Public sector is not performing well

(c) The largest producing sector-agriculture is in private sector

(d) The ratio of growth of private sector has been more than that of the public sector.

30. The share of public sector in national product during the past four decades has been:

(a) Rising (b) Declining
(c) Stagnant (d) Cannot say.

31. All small-scale industry is one in which capital investment does not exceed:

(a) Rs. 2 lakhs (b) Rs. 5 lakhs
(c) Rs. 10 lakhs (d) Rs. 60 lakhs.

32. A long unit is defined as a unit with capital investment of:

(a) Rs. 1 lakh (b) 1.5 lakh
(c) Rs. 1.75 lakh (d) Rs. 5.00 lakh.

33. Life Insurance Corporation is an example of

(a) Development bank (b) Commercial bank
(c) Investment bank (d) Co-operative bank.

34. Find the odd one out:

(a) Punjab National Bank
(b) Bank of Baroda
(c) State Bank of India
(d) Unit Trust of India.

35. Find the odd one at:

(a) Reserve Bank of India
(b) State Bank of India
(c) Bank of India
(d) New Bank of India.

36. Convertibility clause in the loan agreements with financial institutions was introduced in:

(a) 1972 (b) 1976
(c) 1980 (d) 1984.

37. The opex institution in the field of industrial finance of
    (a) Reserve Bank of India
    (b) Industrial Development Bank of India
    (c) Industrial Finance Corporation
    (d) Industrial Credit and Investment Corporation of India.

38. The Industrial Development Bank of India is:
    (a) A private shareholders bank
    (b) An Autonomous public sector institution
    (c) Owned by the Reserve Bank of India
    (d) Managed by the State Bank of India.

39. The major share of financial assistance extended by development banks and investment banks goes to:
    (a) Private sector (b) Public sector
    (c) Joint sector (d) Co-operative sector.

40. The poverty line is defined as:
    (a) The line of minimum calorie intake for bare subsistence
    (b) The line of minimum food intake
    (c) The line of minimum cloth consumption
    (d) The line of maximum cloth consumption.

41. During the British rule in India, India's foreign trade was characterised by
    (a) Large exports of handicrafts
    (b) Large imports of handicrafts
    (c) Large exports of agricultural products
    (d) Large imports of agricultural products.

42. India's first five year plan was launched on:
    (a) January 26,1950 (b) August 15, 1950
    (c) October 2, 1950 (d) April 1,1951.

43. India's fourth five year plan convered the period,
    (a) 1966-71 (b) 1967-72
    (c) 1969-74 (d) 1970-75.

44. India's sixth five year convered the plan:

(a) 1975-80 (b) 1977-82
(c) 1978-83 (d) 1980-85.

45. What is the contribution of agriculture to national income in India?

(a) 44% (b) 50%
(c) 33% (d) 30%.

46. Which of the following factors do we measure the economic growth of India?

(a) Changes in the growth of population
(b) Changes in growth of national product
(c) Changes in the growth of consumption
(d) None of these.

47. The share of agriculture of in India's national income has been:

(a) Increasing (b) Declining
(c) The same (d) Not change.

48. India's major imports consist of

(a) Industrial manufactured goods
(b) Raw material
(c) Agricultural products
(d) Only (a) and (b).

49. Which of the following are the factors responsible for keeping low rate of investment in the Indian economy?

(a) Inadequacy of saving
(b) Non-fulfilment of saving
(c) Failure of the public sector
(d) Inadequacy of the mixed economy
(e) All of these.

50. In which part the Indian budget is divided?

(a) Revenue budget (b) Capital budget
(c) Neither of these (d) Both of these.

ANSWERS

1.	(d)	2.	(d)	3.	(c)	4.	(d)
5.	(c)	6.	(b)	7.	(d)	8.	(b)
9.	(d)	10.	(d)	11.	(b)	12.	(d)
13.	(d)	14.	(d)	15.	(b)	16.	(d)
17.	(d)	18.	(c)	19.	(b)	20.	(c)
21.	(b)	22.	(b)	23.	(d)	24.	(c)
25.	(b)	26.	(d)	27.	(b)	28.	(a)
29.	(c)	30.	(a)	31.	(a)	32.	(b)
33.	(d)	34.	(c)	35.	(d)	36.	(a)
37.	(a)	38.	(b)	39.	(b)	40.	(a)
41.	(a)	42.	(c)	43.	(d)	44.	(d)
45.	(c)	46.	(b)	47.	(b)	48.	(b)
49.	(e)	50.	(d)				

SET 8
ASSESS YOURSELF

1. National income ordinarily means
   (a) Gross National Product at market prices
   (b) Net Product at market prices
   (c) Gross national product at factor cost
   (d) Net National Product at factor cost.

2. "National income as the aggregate net product of, and the sale source of, payment for all the agents of production" has been defined by
   (a) P.C. Pigou (b) Alfred Marshall
   (c) Lionell Robbins (d) Dusenbery.

3. The difference between gross domestic product and net domestic product equals
   (a) Transfer of payments
   (b) Depreciation Cost
   (c) Indirect taxes
   (d) Subsidies.

4. The total income earned in any given year by the owners of productive sources is measured by
   (a) Personal income
   (b) Disposable income
   (c) Gross national product
   (d) National income.

5. In calculating a country's GNP at market prices one of the following is not included.
   (a) Wages and laborious before tax
   (b) Indirect taxes
   (c) Bonus to the employees
   (d) Depreciation allowances.

6. Match the following
   (1) Factor cost
   (2) Market prices
   (3) Gross domestic product
   (4) Gross national product
   (5) Total domestic expenditure

   Definition
   (i) Total goods and services available
   (ii) Total output of goods and services in a country
   (iii) Total spending on home and foreign goods
   (iv) Cost in terms of payments to factors of production
   (v) Actual expenditure in terms of prices paid for goods and services

	1	2	3	4	5
(a)	(iv)	(v)	(ii)	(i)	(iii)
(b)	(iii)	(ii)	(i)	(iv)	(v)
(c)	(v)	(ii)	(i)	(i)	(iii)
(d)	(v)	(i)	(iii)	(ii)	(iv).

7. Which of the following equations is wrong?
   (a) National income= Effective demand
   (b) National income=gross national product
   (c) National income=consumption investment
   (d) National income=consumption saving.

8. Which of the following will directly increase in GNP?
   (a) A rise in the market price
   (b) A surplus in budget
   (c) An increase in investment
   (d) A deficit in budget.

9. If C-20 + 0.6Y, what must be the investment if the equilibrium level of income is Rs. 300 croces?
   (a) Rs. 10 crores (b) Rs. 100 crores
   (c) Rs. 1000 crores (d) Rs. 150crores.

10. The best method of computing national income is:
   (a) Product method
   (b) Income method
   (c) Expenditure method
   (d) Combination of income and production method.

11. On the basis of information given in question No. 21 the net national expenditure will be
   (a) Rs. 74, 000 m (b) Rs. 66,000 m
   (c) Rs. 60,000 m (d) Rs. 14,000 m.

12. What should be substituted for x and Y in the following equation?
   GNP at market prices-GNP at factor cost-x+y
   (a) Indirect taxes, zero
   (b) Indirect taxes, subsidies
   (c) Subsidies, indirect taxes
   (d) Zero, subsidies.

13. Which of the following is not, by definition, equal to national income?
   (a) National output (b) National expenditure
   (c) National product (d) National wealth.

14. Which of the following is a transfer payment?
   (a) Payment made to housewife
   (b) Pocket allowance to children
   (c) Maintenance allownances to old parents
   (d) All of the above.

15. Is GNP is 16% higher than the last years and the rate of inflation is 9%, production in the economy has grown by
   (a) 4% (b) 5%
   (c) 6% (d) 7%.

16. 'Value added' in the following illustration will equal -------------from the following data

(a) Rs. 500 (b) Rs. 400

(c) Rs. 650 (d) Rs. 250.

17. The difference between gross national product and gross domestic product is equal to

(a) Gross domestic investment

(b) Net foreign investment

(c) Net imports

(d) Net factor income from abroad.

18. Net domestic product at factor cost equals net domestic product at market prices:

(a) Plus subsidies-indirect taxes

(b) Minus sub-ind. sub

(c) Minus subsidies

(d) Plus indirect taxes.

19. When gross investment is positive, net investment

(a) Is the highest

(b) Is zero

(c) Is positive

(d) Can be either positive or negative.

20. " Disposable income" doesnot include

(a) Business transfer payment

(b) Social security benefits

(c) Corporate dividends

(d) Personal income.

21. Corporate profits included in disposable personal income source?

(a) Dividends

(b) Indirect taxes

(c) Capital consumption allowances

(d) Corporate income taxes.

22. Circular flow of income in a two sector model implies:
    (a) Payments from household to firms
    (b) Payments from household to household
    (c) Payments from households to house
    (d) None of the above.

23. Which of the following is not included in calculating gross national product of an economy?
    (a) Wages and salaries before tax
    (b) Depreciation allowances
    (c) Indirect taxes
    (d) Subsidies.

24. The consolidated government budget differs from the union budget by:
    (a) Imports
    (b) State and local government expenditures
    (c) Union tax receipts
    (d) Inter-governmental transfers.

25. In national income terms, which of the following plays the important rate in the what economic activity?
    (a) The level of taxation
    (b) Realised investment
    (c) Planned saving
    (d) Factor mobility.

26. Which one of the following is a transfer income ?
    (a) The salary of an M.P.
    (b) The company dividends to share holders
    (c) Rents from house property
    (d) Unempoyment allowance.

27. For the study of the long term growth of the economy we use
    (a) Real GNP (b) Transfer payments
    (c) Per capita income (d) Disposable income.

28. Double counting has the effect of
    (a) Under estimating national product
    (b) Over estimating national product
    (c) Distorting national product
    (d) Misleading conclusions about national income.

29. The smallest national income accounting aggregate is usually
    (a) P1 (b) GNP
    (c) DP1 (d) Nd1.

30. A firm in a two sector model is essentially a unit of
    (a) Consumption (b) Production
    (c) Investment (d) None of the above.

31. Which of the following is not a method of estimating GNP?
    (a) The value added approach
    (b) Product approach
    (c) Income approach
    (d) The financial approach.

32. Depreciation is loss of the value of
    (a) Capital assets (b) Stocks
    (c) Intermediate goods (d) Final goods.

33. Deflator technique is used for adjusting
    (a) Price rise only
    (b) Price fall only
    (c) Price rise and fall both
    (d) Price rise and fall together.

34. In calculating GNP which of the following should be excluded?
    (a) Rental incomes
    (b) Interest payments
    (c) Dividends
    (d) Goverment transfer payments.

35. The condition of equilibrium in a four sector model is
    (a) S+T+M=G+T+M (b) S+T=G+1
    (c). S=1 (d). T=G.

36. GNP is Rs. 600 crores and NNP is Rs. 475 crores, therefore depreciation is
    (a) Rs. 100 (b) Rs. 175
    (c) Rs. 50 (d) Rs. 125.

37. The difference between GNP and NNP is accounted for by
    (a) Transfer payments (b) Capital consumption
    (c) Value added (d) Stock apperciation.

38. NNP at market prices and NNP at factor costs will be equal when there is
    (a) No direct tax
    (b) No indirect tax
    (c) No subsidy
    (d) No indirect tax and no subsidy.

39. Which of the following is not one of the problems in calculation of national income?
    (a) Double counting
    (b) Improper records
    (c) Difference in the incomes of individuals
    (d) Problems of exclusion and inclusion.

40. In the sector accounts, government purchases of imports appear in part a receipt of
    (a) The household sector
    (b) The government sector
    (c) The business sector
    (d) None of these.

41. The foreign sector
    (a) Net exports are negative when
    (b) Net investment is positive
    (c) Exports are exceeded by imports
    (d) Imports are exceeded by exports.

42. In a closed economy model one of the sectors below is not considered which?
(a) Households (b) Firms
(c) Government (d). Foreign trade.

43. National dividend is that part of the objective income of the community, including of course income derived from abroad, which can be measured in money. Who said it?
(a) Marshall (b) Hicks
(c) Ricardo (d) Robinson.

44. National product at market prices is higher than national product at factor cast by the amount of
(a) Subsidies
(b) Indirect taxes
(c) Indirect taxes plus subsidies
(d) Indirect taxes minus subsidies.

45. The important leakages in the circular flow of income are as follows except one. which?
(a) Saving
(b) Imports
(c) Government expenditure
(d) Taxes.

46. Subsidies to business increase the figure of
(a) NNP at market price (b) P1
(c) NP (d) D1.

47. Which of the following measures does not include final goods and services?
(a) GNP (b) NNP
(c) Disposable income (d) National income.
(e) None of the above

48. A sells all his output to B; B sells for Rs. 60 to C, B's value added is equal to A's. So A sells to B for
(a) Rs. 20 (b) Rs. 30
(c) Rs. 40 (d) Rs. 60.

49. Imports into a country generate income for
    (a) Domestic manufactures
    (b) Government
    (c) Traders
    (d) Foreign products.

50. National income total reveals
    (a) The Spending Side (b) The Production Side
    (c) The Distributive Side (d) The Investment Side.

ANSWERS

1.	(d)	2.	(d)	3.	(b)	4.	(d)
5.	(d)	6.	(a)	7.	(b)	8.	(c)
9.	(b)	10.	(d)	11.	(b)	12.	(c)
13.	(d)	14.	(d)	15.	(d)	16.	(d)
17.	(a)	18.	(d)	19.	(d)	20.	(a)
21.	(a)	22.	(b)	23.	(b)	24.	(b)
25.	(d)	26.	(a)	27.	(c)	28.	(b)
29.	(c)	30.	(b)	31.	(d)	32.	(a)
33.	(c)	34.	(d)	35.	(a)	36.	(d)
37.	(b)	38.	(d)	39.	(c)	40.	(d)
41.	(d)	42.	(d)	43.	(a)	44.	(d)
45.	(c)	46.	(a)	47.	(c)	48.	(b)
49.	(d)	50.	(a)				

SET 9
ASSESS YOURSELF

1. The economic analysis expects the consumers to behave in a manner which is
   (a) Rational (b) Irrational
   (c) Emotional (d) Indifferent.
2. Consumer goods means
   (a) All goods other than free goods used by consumers in order to earn their living
   (b) All goods other than free goods whose use directly Stisfied consumer wants
   (c) All commodities for which there is a high demand by all types of consumers
   (d) All the factories and mines used by the commodity to satisfy their wants.
3. If a consumer buy a unit of commodity without much hesitation it is regarded as
   (a) Marginal
   (b) Extra marginal
   (c) Intra marginal
   (d) Consumers preference.
4. Which of the following concepts are most closely associated with Alfred Marshall?
   (a) Marginal utility theory
   (b) Price mecnanism under monopoly
   (c) Modern theory of wage
   (d) Interest theory.

5. Marginal utility curve is always
   (a) Rising (b) Falling
   (c) Parallel to x-axis (d) Parallel to Y-axis.

6. The shape of marginal utility curve for a normal good and rational consumer is
   (a) Upward sloping (b) Horizontal
   (c) Downward sloping (d) Vertical.

7. The total utility is maximum when
   (a) M.U. is zero (b) A.U. is the highest
   (c) M.U. is the highest (d) M.U. is equal to A.U.

8. The falling part of a T.U. curve shows
   (a) Increasing marginal utility
   (b) Decreasing marginal utility
   (c) Increasing marginal utility
   (d) None of the above.

9. MU of n units is found by the following formula:
   (a) Tu/n (b) Tu×n
   (c) Tun-Tu(n-1) (d) P+n.

10. "Jtils" is a term used
    (a) By Marshall in demand theory
    (b) By Walras to measure cardinal utility
    (c) To mean marginal utility
    (d) None of the above.

11. An activity directed towards the statisfaction of wants is called
    (a) Production (b) Utility
    (c) Consumption (d) None of these.

12. A consumer's demand curve can be obtained from
    (a) Income consumption curve
    (b) Engel's curve
    (c) Price-consumption curve
    (d) None of these.

13. A farmer has x acres under wheat cultivation and decides that he will devote x+1 acres to wheat the additional area is known in economic analysis as the
    (a) Cultivable unit (b) Profitable unit
    (c) Marginal unit (d) Economic unit.

14. Goods other than free goods which, when used directly satisfy consumer want's is called
    (a) Producers goods (b) Free goods
    (c) Intermediate goods (d) Consumer's goods.

15. 'Marginal utility approach' was finalised by
    (a) J.R. Hicks (b) Alfred Marshall
    (c) J.S. Mill (d) A.C. Pigou.

16. When relating a diminishing marginal utility curve the OX and OY axis measure respectively
    (a) Units of the commodity price
    (b) Units of the commodity and revenue
    (c) Units of the commodity and price of the substitude
    (d) Units of the commodity and marginal utility.

17. The law of equi-marginal utility is called by several other names which one of the following would be a good
    (a) Law of indifference
    (b) Law of subtitution
    (c) Law of utility and demand
    (d) Law of economy expenditure.

18. Law of diminishing marginal utility applies to:
    (a) Drunkards (b) Misers
    (c) Stamp collectors (d) None of the above.

19. One of the following is the odd one out: which is it?
    (a) Law of substitution
    (b) Theory of diminishing marginal utility
    (c) Indifference curve analysis
    (d) Law of available proportions.

20. The marginal utility curve is
    (a) The demand curve of that commodity
    (b) Parallel to OX axis
    (c) Parallel to OY axis
    (d) Opposite to the demand curve.

21. Diminishing marginal utility means that
    (a) Total utility rises at a constant rate
    (b) Total utility rises, at first then falls
    (c) Total utility rises, but at a decreasing rate
    (d) Total utility remains the same.

22. The area which lies under the demand curve for a given good measures
    (a) Marginal utility
    (b) Total utility
    (c) Disutility
    (d) Marginal cost of production.

23. Which of the following creates time utility?
    (a) Farmer (b) Carpenter
    (c) Trader (d) Driver.

24. Which of the following assumptions do economists always make about consumers?
    (a) They make rational decisions in the market
    (b) They cannot spend more than their income
    (c) They are all daily wage earners
    (d) Their tastes operate in the same direction.

25. An inferior goods is inferior
    (a) For every consumer
    (b) For same consumers and not for others
    (c) For most consumers
    (d) For the community as a whole.

26. The concept marginal utility is useful for explaining demand-water paradox" this statement is
    (a) Absolutely correct (b) Partially correct
    (c) Absolutely wrong (d) None of these.

27. MU curve will be below x-axis when
    (a) MU curve is positive (b) Curve is negative
    (c) MU is zero (d) MU is constant.

28. As a consumer increases his consumption of accommodity of the total utility he derives from its consumption increase but at a diminishing rate. This is;
    (a) A statement of fact
    (b) An economic law
    (c) A hypothesis
    (d) None of the above.

29. A consumer reaches equilibirium at the point where
    (a) MU=P (b) MU< P
    (c) MU>P (d) TU=P.

30. Match the following.
    (i) Total utility
    (ii) Marginal utility
    (iii) Law of equimarginal utility
    A. Falling
    B. Concave to x-axis
    C. Consumer's surplus
    D. More rupee spent on x and y commodity
    (a) (i,A)
    (b) (iB) (ii,C) (iii,A)
    (c) (i,B), (ii,A)< (iiiD)
    (d) (i,D), (ii, C), (iii,B).

31. Utility is
    (a) A subjective concept
    (b) A moral concept
    (c) An objective concept
    (d) A neutral concept.

32. At the saturation point of commodity Y the MU is
    (a) Positive (b) Zero
    (c) Negative (d) None of the above.

33. The term optimum allocation on consumer's expenditure on various goods and services is used in
    (a) Law of demand
    (b) Giffen Paradox
    (c) Law of equi-marginal utility
    (d) Law of diminishing marginal utility.

34. Utility has relevance to
    (a) Usefulness
    (b) Expected satisfaction
    (c) Social sanction
    (d) None of the above.

35. The fact that each want is non-satiable given rise to
    (a) The law of substitution
    (b) The indefference curve analysis
    (c) The law of substitution
    (d) None of the above.

36. A falling MU curve illustrates
    (a) The principle of diminishing marginal utility
    (b) The principle of diminishing marginal rate of substitution
    (c) The principle of equi-marginal utility
    (d) None of these.

37. The law of equi-marginal utility tables that if price of commodity falls
    (a) More units of it will be bought
    (b) Less units of it will be bought
    (c) Same units of it will be bought
    (d) Nothing of it will be bought.

38. Maximisation of total utility is an assumption of a consumer analysis, that is
    (a) Indifference curve approach
    (b) Demand analysis
    (c) Utility analysis
    (d) Marginal utility analysis.

39. The curve which first moves upwards then downwards naturally is
    (a) Marginal utility curve
    (b) Average utility curve
    (c) Total utility curve
    (d) Demand curve.

40. Which of the following is called as the Gossen's first law?
    (a) Law of substitution
    (b) The law of equi-marginal utility
    (c) The law of diminishing utility
    (d) The law of indifference.

41. Marginal utility has no place in a ordinal theory because it is
    (a) Introspective
    (b) Subjective
    (c) Not of servable
    (d) Additive.

42. When relating a diminishing marginal utility curve the ox and OY axis measure repectively
    (a) Units of commodity and price
    (b) Units of commodity and income
    (c) Units of commodity and price of a substitution
    (d) Units of the commodity and marginal utility.

43. Ordianal approach is based on
    (a) Law of maximum satisfaction
    (b) Utility could not be measured in cardinal numbers
    (c) Utility could not be measured in in ordinal numbers
    (d) Utility can be measured.

44. The utility function is best represented as
    (a) Utility = price
    (b) Utility t-1- U (price t1)
    (c) Utility X+Y = U(price) quantity X+Y
    (d) Utility = U (quantity).

45. The price which a consumer would be willing to pay for a commodity equal to his
   (a) Total utility
   (b) Marginal utility
   (c) Average utility
   (d) Does not have relation to any one of thfese.

46. Total utility curve
   (a) Always rises
   (b) Always falls
   (c) First falls and then rises
   (d) First rises and then falls.

47. Economists associated with the development of indifference curve analysis are
   (a) J.R. Hicks and R.G.D Allen
   (b) J.R. Hicks and Robbins
   (c) J.R Hicks and R.G.D Allen
   (d) J.R Hicks and Leon Walras.

48. Which of the following is one of the assumption of the indifference curve analysis?
   (a) Cardinal utility
   (b) Ordinal utility
   (c) Indeqendent utility
   (d) Constant marginal utility.

49. An indifference curve is always:
   (a) Concave to the origin
   (b) Canvex to the origin
   (c) A vertical straight line
   (d) A horizontal straight line.

50. An indifference curve always
   (a) Slopes downward from left to right
   (b) Slopes upwards from right to left
   (c) Slopes upwards from right to left
   (d) Is parallel to x-axis.

ANSWERS

1.	(a)	2.	(b)	3.	(c)	4.	(a)
5.	(b)	6.	(c)	7.	(a)	8.	(d)
9.	(c)	10.	(b)	11.	(c)	12.	(c)
13.	(c)	14.	(d)	15.	(b)	16.	(d)
17.	(a)	18.	(d)	19.	(d)	20.	(a)
21.	(c)	22.	(b)	23.	(c)	24.	(a)
25.	(b)	26.	(a)	27.	(b)	28.	(c)
29.	(a)	30.	(c)	31.	(a)	32.	(b)
33.	(c)	34.	(b)	35.	(a)	36.	(a)
37.	(a)	38.	(d)	39.	(c)	40.	(c)
41.	(d)	42.	(d)	43.	(b)	44.	(d)
45.	(b)	46.	(d)	47.	(c)	48.	(b)
49.	(b)	50.	(a)				

SET 10
ASSESS YOURSELF

1. The most important of the variables which affect saving was, according to Keynes
   (a) Employment,
   (b) Income
   (c) Short term interest rates
   (d) Demand elasticity.

2. Total consumption expenditure in an economy does not include one of the following
   (a) Consumption expenditure of households
   (b) Investment expenditure of firms
   (c) Government expenditure
   (d) None of the above.

3. Total nation investment consist of:
   (a) Gross domestic capital information
   (b) Change in stocks
   (c) Export less imports
   (d) All of the above.

4. A household in a two sector model is essentially a unit of
   (a) Consumption (b) Production
   (c) Investment (d) None of the above.

5. National product at market prices incorporates
   (a) Prices which buyers actually pay
   (b) Payments made to the factor owner

(c) Costs incurred in producing goods and services
(d) Costs minus subsidies.

6. Which of the following is not an act of investment
   (a) Consumption of a factory building
   (b) Work in progress
   (c) Increase in stocks
   (d) Issue of new shares.

7. When less output is consumed than produced during a given income period, national wealth
   (a) Increases
   (b) Remain some changed as there is no relationship
   (c) Decreases
   (d) May increase or decrease.

8. Who of the following Indian economists scientifically estimated the nation income of India
   (a) Dadabhai Naoroji (b) Dr. K.N. Raj
   (c) Dr. V.K. R.V. Rao (d) Dr. Vakil.

9. The largest contribution in value term to India's GNP is made by
   (a) Agriculture
   (b) Construction
   (c) Organised industries
   (d) Unorganised industries.

10. National product curve net prices is higher than national product at constant prices during a period of
    (a) Rising prices (b) Falling prices
    (c) Stable prices (d) Changing costs.

11. The purchase of a new home is included in the GNP as a part of
    (a) Capital consumption allowance
    (b) Personal consumption expenditure
    (c) Investment
    (d) Personal saving.

12. National prices product at market prices is higher than national product at factor cost by the amount of
    (a) Indirect taxes
    (b) Subsidies
    (c) Indirect taxes plus subsidies
    (d) Indirect taxes minus subsidies.

13. Expenditure on defence is an item of
    (a) Private investment
    (b) Public investment
    (c) Private consumption
    (d) Public consumption.

14. If value added at different stages are added, the total will
    (a) Equal the value of final product
    (b) Overestimate the value of the final product
    (c) Underestimate the value of the final product
    (d) Misrepresent the value of the final product.

15. Which of the following is not included while estimating national income through income method
    (a) Rent (b) Mixed income
    (c) Pension (d) Undistributed profit.

16. Which of the following is not included in a country's capital stock?
    (a) Company debentures and shares
    (b) Raw materials in the hands of producers
    (c) Docks and harbours
    (d) Finish goods in the hands of producers.

17. In the light of the final product concept' goods produced by firm A and sold to firm B for further processing
    (a) Is to be included in product
    (b) Is to benot included in product
    (c) Is to be included to the extant of value added by A
    (d) Is to be included at a lower value.

18. In an economy whose productive capacity is expanding
    (a) DP1 exceeds P1
    (b) Gross private domestic investment exceeds depreciotion
    (c) NNP exceeds GNP
    (d) Money GNP is rising.

19. Most of the macro-economic variables are
    (a) Stock variables
    (b) Flow variables
    (c) Stock and flow variables
    (d) None of the above.

20. If depreciation of capital assets is ignored from national income, it will rebuilt in
    (a) Depletion of capital assets
    (b) Overestimation of national income
    (c) Exaggerating the value of capital goods
    (d) Underestimating the value of output.

21. The total sales of all firms in an economy in a given year is
    (a) The same as gross national product
    (b) Equal to that of national income
    (c) More than gross national product
    (d) Less than gross national product.

22. The most important injections in the circular flow of income are as follows except one. Which is?
    (a) Investments
    (b) Exports
    (c) Government expenditure
    (d) Taxes.

23. Which of the following is not investment?
    (a) Expenditure on purchase of capital goods
    (b) Expenditure on purchase of foodgrains
    (c) Expenditure on expansion of the plant
    (d) Expenditure on setting up a new plant.

24. The gross output of a firm minus material and services which it by from other firms is an estimate of the firm's
    (a) Gross expenditure (b) Net porofit
    (c) Opportunity cost (d) Value added.

25. Transaction in financial assets cause
    (a) An increase in national income
    (b) A decrease in national income
    (c) Keep national income unaffected
    (d) Increase national income in the future.

26. National product at market prices is used for knowing
    (a) Changes in its industrial origin
    (b) The growth of the economy
    (c) Changes in factor payments
    (d) Changes in the regional distribution of income.

27. Purchase of a new dwelling is an act of
    (a) Instant consumption (b) Gradual consumption
    (c) Investment (d) None of the above.

28. Corporate profit included in the disposable personal income are
    (a) Dividends
    (b) Indirect business taxes
    (c) Capital consumption allowance
    (d) Undistributed corporate profits.

29. Changes in stocks are a result of
    (a) Deliberate decisions by manufactures
    (b) Deliberate decisions by shopkeepers
    (c) Failure of sellers to sell good
    (d) Deviations between supply and demand.

30. Assume an economy with less than full employment in which there is an increase in aggregate demand. A likely immediate result will be
    (a) An increase in holding of stocks of some goods
    (b) A reduction in holding of stocks of some goods

(c) A fall in investment
(d) A drastic fall in employment in the distributivetrades.

31. The secondary sector of Indian economy does not include
(a) Manufacturing
(b) Construction
(c) Mining and quarrying
(d) Electricity, gas and water supply.

32. Transfer payment because they increase the income of the receipt
(a) Are included in national product
(b) Are excluded from national product
(c) Contributed to national product
(d) Are partly included in national product.

33. Imports into a country generate income for
(a) Domestic manufactures
(b) Government
(c) Traders
(d) Foreign producers.

34. Progressive income taxes will redistribute income only if
(a) There is private ownership of wealth
(b) Incomes are unequal
(c) There is no evasion of tax
(d) Land is owned by the state.

35. The basic theoretical structure in macro-economics is
(a) Aggregate demand
(b) Aggregate supply
(c) Circular flow of income
(d) Consumption and invesment.

36. Which of the following paris is correct:

(A)	April to March	(i)	A UN year
(B)	January to December	(ii)	A calendar year
(C)	July to June	(iii)	A financial year

(a) (A,i) (b) (B,iii)
(c) (A,iii) (d) (C,ii).

37. A growing country is one with
(a) Rising GNP at constant prices
(b) Constant GNP at constant prices
(c) Rising GNP at current prices
(d) None of these.

38. Which Social Accounting statement can tell you regarding are the inter-relation ships between specified industries?
(a) Flow of funds
(b) Balance of payments
(c) Input-output table
(d) National income and unemployment.

39. A major part of a country's output is normally used for
(a) Private consumption
(b) Public consumption
(c) Investments
(d) Exports.

40. Which of the following is not included while estimating national income through income method?
(a) Wages (b) Indirect taxes
(c) Dividends (d) Direct taxes.

41. The national investment consists of
(a) Gross domestic fixed capital formation
(b) Change in stocks
(c) Export less imports
(d) All the three.

42. Which of the following is not a source of aggregate demand?
(a) X-M (b) C
(c) G (d). S.

43. For a study at the long term growth of the economy we use
(a) Real GNP
(b) Money GNP

(c) Per capita income
(d) Property of the individual.

44. The GNP at factor cost at the 1970-71 prices for the year 1980-81 was estimated as

(a) Rs. 77,414 crores (b) Rs. 87,414 crores
(c) Rs. 57,414 crores (d) None of these.

45. Total business saving is the composition of

(a) Capital consumption allowance
(b) Dividends
(c) Undistributed corporate profits
(d) Corporate profit taxes.

46. A negative contribution to aggregate demand is sometimes made by the following sector

(a) Business (b) Household
(c) Foreign (d) Government.

47. A 'refrigerator' operating in a chemists shop as an example of

(a) Intermediate good (b) Final good
(c) Foreign (d) Consumer's good.

48. The total sales of all firms in an economy in a given year is

(a) Less than gross national product
(b) Equal to that of national income
(c) More than gross national product
(d) The same as gross national product.

49. The workers were classified as 'productive and unproductive on the productivity context by

(a) Kavid Ricardo (b) J.S. Mill
(c) Adam Smith (d) Karl Marx.

50. The general theory of employment, interest and money in 1936 was written by

(a) Ragnar Nurkse (b) J.S. Mill
(c) J.B. Say (d) J.M. Keynes.

ANSWERS

1.	(b)	2.	(d)	3.	(d)	4.	(a)
5.	(a)	6.	(d)	7.	(a)	8.	(c)
9.	(a)	10.	(a)	11.	(c)	12.	(d)
13.	(d)	14.	(a)	15.	(c)	16.	(a)
17.	(b)	18.	(b)	19.	(c)	20.	(b)
21.	(c)	22.	(d)	23.	(b)	24.	(d)
25.	(c)	26.	(c)	27.	(a)	28.	(a)
29.	(d)	30.	(b)	31.	(c)	32.	(a)
33.	(d)	34.	(b)	35.	(c)	36.	(b)
37.	(d)	38.	(c)	39.	(c)	40.	(c)
41.	(c)	42.	(a)	43.	(b)	44.	(d)
45.	(d)	46.	(a)	47.	(d)	48.	(b)
49.	(c)	50.	(c)				

SET 11
ASSESS YOURSELF

1. If the quantity of commodity demanded does not change when its price change, the demand curve for this commodity is
   (a) Negatively stopped (b) Positively stopped
   (c) Horizontal (d) Vertical.

2. Which of the following does not have uniform elasticity of demand at all points?
   (a) A vertical demand curve
   (b) A horizontal demand
   (c) A rectangular hypoerbola demand curve
   (d) A downward sloping demand.

3. Cross elasticity of demand for patrol is the responsiveness of demand for petrol
   (a) Prices of car (b) Price of petrol
   (c) Change in income (d) None of the above.

4. If more is demanded at the same prices or the same quantity is demanded at a higher price this is known as
   (a) Extension of demand (b) Contraction of demand
   (c) Increase in demand (d) Decrease in deman.

5. The price elasticity of demand for a good a is minus 2. What is the change in price that will induce a 10 % fall in the quantity demanded?
   (a) -20 % (b) 5 %
   (c) +20 % (d) + 2 %.

6. Following reduction in price of a commodity by 5 per cent total expenditure in that commodity falls by 3 per cent. Demand in this case can be described as

(a) Inelastic (b) Perfectly inelastic
(c) Elastic (d) Perfectly elastic.

7. The coefficient of price elasticity in demand between two points is called

(a) Income elasticity (b) Arc elasticity
(c) Cross elasticity (d) None of the above.

8. On a straight-line demand curve, elasticity of element at mid-point of the curve is:

(a) 2 (b) 1/2
(c) 1 (d) 4.

9. Demand for electricity is

(a) Inelastic (b) Elastic
(c) Less elastic (d) None of these.

10. A high value of cross-elasticity indicates that the two commodities curve

(a) Very good substitute
(b) Poor substitute
(c) Good complements
(d) Poor complements.

11. If cross elasticity of one commodity for another turns out to be zero, it means they are-

(a) Cross substitutes
(b) Good complements
(c) Completely unrelated
(d) None of these.

12. An increase in the price of a commodity when demand is inelastic causes the tefidd expenditures of consumers of the commodity to:

(a) Increase (b) Decrease
(c) Remain unchanged (d) Any of the above.

13. In case the two commodities are complements
   (a) Positive (b) Unitary
   (c) Negative (d) Infinite.

14. A commodity having a number of uses will face a demand which is
   (a) Unit elastic (b) Inelastic
   (c) Elastic (d) None of these.

15. Two commodities are considered to be perfect substitutes for cash other if the elasticity of substitution is
   (a) Positive (b) Negative
   (c) Zero (d) Infinite.

16. Elasticity (E) expressed by the formulam 1> E > 0 is
   (a) Perfect elastic
   (b) Relatively elastic
   (c) Completely elastic
   (d) Relatively inelastic.

17. A straight line, downward sloping demand curve implies that, as price fells, the elasticity of demand
   (a) IS zero (b) Remains same
   (c) Decreases (d) Increases.

18. If the quantity demanded of commodity is plotted against the price of a substitute goods, certerins paribus, the curve is expected to be
   (a) Vertical (b) Positively sloped
   (c) Horizontal (d) Negatively sloped.

19. Of the following commodities which has the lowest elasticity of demand-
   (a) Car (b) Salt
   (c) Tea (d) Houses.

20. If R point bisects the demand curve in two equal points, then elasticity equals
   (a) Zero (b) Five
   (c) Two (d) One

21. A fall in price of a commodity whose demand curve in a rectangular hyperbola causes total expenditure on the commodity is
   (a) Increase (b) Decrease
   (c) Remain unchanged (d) None of the above.

22. The horizontal demand curve for a commodity shows that its demand is
   (a) Highly elastic (b) Perfectly inelastic
   (c) Perfectly elastic (d) Moderately elastic.

23. Suppose your income increases by 10% and demand for commodity increases by 10% then the income elasticity of demand is
   (a) Negative (b) Positive
   (c) Zero (d) Infinity.

24. In the case of a superior commodity,the income elasticity of demand is
   (a) Positive (b) Zero
   (c) Negative (d) Infinite.

25. In which case the elasticity shows by the different points of a curve is the same?
   (a) A rectangular hyperbola curve
   (b) A straight line curve
   (c) A downward slopling curve
   (d) None of these.

26. A situation where the amount spent by consumers on acommodity in constent when pricechanges, is known as-
   (a) Equilibrium
   (b) Perfect elasticity
   (c) Uniteing elasticity
   (d) Backward sloping demand.

27. With an increases in income, a consumer is expected to buy more of
   (a) An inferior goods
   (b) A superior goods

(c) A normal for superior goods
(d) All kinds of goods.

28. Which of the following is the method of measuring elasticity of demand when changes in price of commodity is substantial?
(a) Percentage method
(b) Point method
(c) Are method
(d) None of these.

29. Assuming that the prices of kerosene stove crowed gas stove bolk within the same range the cross elasticity of demand between them would be
(a) Very low (b) High
(c) Infinite (d) Low.

30. A country is advised to develop (reduce external value of) its currency only when its export face
(a) Inelastic demand in foreign markets
(b) Elastic demand in foreign markets
(c) Unit elastic demand in foreign markets
(d) None of these.

31. At a point the middle of a straight line demand curve elasticity of demand is
(a) Less than one (b) Equal to one
(c) More than one (d) Equal to infinity.

32. Elasticity of supply for a positively sloped straight line supply curve that intersects the price exis is
(a) Zero (b) =1
(c) >1 (d) Constant.

33. A demand curve is not related to
(a) The price of the commodity
(b) The time period
(c) The orign of substitutes
(d) A given market.

34. An income demand curve for inferior commodity always slopes
   (a) Upwards to the right
   (b) Backward
   (c) Downwards to the right
   (d) Horizontally.

35. When the law of demand operates the demand curve
   (a) Slopes downward from left to right
   (b) Slopes upward from left to right
   (c) Slopes upward from right to left
   (d) Paraller to horizontal areas.

36. When an individual's income falls (if everything else remains the same) demands for an interior goods:
   (a) Increases
   (b) Decreases
   (c) Remains
   (d) We cannot say without additional information.

37. When both the price of a substitute and the price of a complement of commodity X rise, the demand for X:
   (a) Rises
   (b) Falls
   (c) Remains unchanged
   (d) All of the above are possible.

38. When the price of substitute of commodity X falls, the demand for X:
   (a) Rises (b) Falls
   (c) Remanis unchanged (d) Any of the above.

39. Bread and butter, lamb and mentsauce, illustrate the type of item related demand known as:
   (a) Rival demand (b) Composite demand
   (c) Competitive demand (d) Joint demand.

40. Two goods have to be consumed simultaneously are:
   (a) Identical (b) Complementary
   (c) Substitutes (d) None of these.

41. Which of the following pairs of commodities is an example of Substitutes:
    (a) Coffee and milk
    (b) Diamond and cow
    (c) Pen and ink
    (d) Mustard oil and coconutoil.

42. An exceptional demand curve is one that slops:
    (a) Upward to the right
    (b) Downward to the left
    (c) Upward to the left
    (d) Horizontally.

43. The vertical demand curve for a commodity shows that its demand is:
    (a) Highly elastic (b) Perfectly inelastic
    (c) Family elastic (d) Modertely elastic.

44. Demand for a commodity is elastic when it has:
    (a) Only one use
    (b) Many uses
    (c) Uses which can be postponed
    (d) Uses very essential for the consumer.

45. Income effect operate through an increase:
    (a) In real income
    (b) In many income
    (c) In wages
    (d) In real income because of the fall of price of a commodity.

46. If a two commodity word, if dx is custary elastic, a rise in the price of x ceteris paribus result in:
    (a) Less of 'y' being bought
    (b) More of 'y' being bought
    (c) The same amount of being bought
    (d) Any of the above is possible.

47. In the longer period permitting adjustment demand is likely to be:
    (a) Inelastic (b) Elastic
    (c) Unit elastic (d) Cannot be known.

48. A demand curve when takes the form of a horizontal line parallel to the quantity elastic which is:
    (a) Zero (b) Intinite
    (c) >1 (d) <1.

49. Elasticity of demand is equal to unity while marginal revenue is
    (a) Positive (b) Zero
    (c) Negative (d) Indeterminate.

50. One common definition of luxury goods is goods with an income elasticity
    (a) Greater than one
    (b) Equal to one
    (c) Less than one but more than Zero
    (d) None of these.

ANSWERS

1.	(d)	2.	(d)	3.	(d)	4.	(c)
5.	(c)	6.	(b)	7.	(b)	8.	(c)
9.	(b)	10.	(a)	11.	(c)	12.	(a)
13.	(c)	14.	(c)	15.	(d)	16.	(d)
17.	(d)	18.	(b)	19.	(b)	20.	(d)
21.	(c)	22.	(c)	23.	(b)	24.	(a)
25.	(a)	26.	(a)	27.	(c)	28.	(c)
29.	(c)	30.	(b)	31.	(c)	32.	(c)
33.	(c)	34.	(b)	35.	(a)	36.	(b)
37.	(a)	38.	(b)	39.	(d)	40.	(b)
41.	(d)	42.	(a)	43.	(b)	44.	(b)
45.	(d)	46.	(c)	47.	(b)	48.	(b)
49.	(b)	50.	(a)				

SET 12
ASSESS YOURSELF

1. The special bearer bonds sechme was introduced in India in the year
   (a) 1950 (b) 1981
   (c) 1975 (d) 1985.
2. Octroi is levied and collected by:
   (a) Centre
   (b) State government
   (c) Local bodies
   (d) All the above.
3. The EXIM Bank of India was set up in
   (a) 1980 (b) 1982
   (c) 1983 (d) 1984.
4. Unit Trust of India was set up in the year
   (a) 1962 (b) 1964
   (c) 1966 (d) 1968.
5. The base year in the new series of the wholesale price India(wpi) was been shifted from 1970-71to
   (a) 1980-81 (b) 1981-82
   (c) 1983-84 (d) 1984-85.
6. Over the four decades, starting from 1950-51, India's per capita income in 1980-81 prices has increased by around
   (a) 60% (b) 70%
   (c) 80% (d) 90%.

7. In 1989 agriculture contributed % or the GDP
   (a) 30% (b) 35%
   (c) 39% (d) 40%.

8. In the planning period both saving and investments rates have
   (a) Agriculture
   (b) Commerce
   (c) Industry
   (d) Entrepreneurs.

9. Over the year per head agricultural land had steadily declined in this country was around:
   (a) 7% (b) 8%
   (c) 9% (d) 10%.

10. Over the planning period both saving and investment rates have:
   (a) Fallen (b) Risen
   (c) Remained content (d) Fallen marginally.

11. The target in the First plan had fixed a percent rise in net national product (NNP), but the achievment was percent
   (a) 10,9 (b) 11,18
   (c). 18,11 (d) 12,14.

12. The target in the second plan was to raise NNP by ...... percent but the actual rise NNP was .... precent
   (a) 25, 21-4 (b) 26, 207
   (c) 25, 22-5 (d) 27, 259.

13. During the seventh plan the rise of increase in NNP has been around
   (a) 6% (b) 5.5%
   (c) 5% (d) 4.6%.

14. The investment make in the state sector during the past few decades were around
   (a) 60% (b) 55%
   (c) 45% (d) 40%.

15. India planning is more elected to
    (a) Socialism (b) Fabian society
    (c) Capitalism (d) None of the above.

16. Over the time open of two decades since the inception of planning, the big business houses have been able to increase their assets by
    (a) Three times (b) 5 times
    (c) 7 times (d) More than 10 times.

17. The share of the public sector in the total national output in india is
    (a) More than 50%
    (b) More than 30% but less than 50%
    (c) Less than 25%
    (d) 27%.

18. State capitalism basically implies
    (a) A socialistic economy
    (b) A capitalist economy
    (c) A mixed economy
    (d) None of the above.

19. In India, the mixed economy framework has tended to fovour
    (a) Relatively rich (b) Realatively poor
    (c) Poorest of the poor (d) All section of society.

20. India still remains one of the most underdeveloped nations in terms of
    (a) Natural resources
    (b) The availbability of capital
    (c) Per capita income
    (d) Per capita expenditure.

21. The third plan contemplated a percent increases in NNP but it rare merely by %
    (a) 28,9.5 (b) 29,10.6
    (c) 30,11.7 (d) 31,12.1.

22. The planning expereince in INDIA tells us that planning in India had remained
    (a) Inadequate (b) Adqaute
    (c) A dynamic (d) A static one.

23. Occupational distrubtion of population in India during the planning period
    (a) Changed significantly
    (b) Remained almost unchanged
    (c) Marked a progressive note
    (d) Marked a retardation.

24. The balanced growth theory was propounded by
    (a) H. Leibenstien (b) J,viner
    (c) A.K.Sen (d) R. Nurkse.

25. Who was propounded the doctrine or unbalanced growth
    (a) R.Nursk
    (b) Albert O Hirschman
    (c) Rosenstein Rodan
    (d) H.Myint.

26. The major problem of capital formation crops up as a conflict between
    (a) The investment and savings
    (b) The GNP and NNP
    (c) The socialistic and Capitalistic way of planning
    (d) The preference for current consumption and need to save.

27. The demand for capital in essence is a
    (a) Direct Demand
    (b) Reciprocal demand
    (c) Derived demand
    (d) Complemantary demand.

28. What use the obstacle to expend the merket
    (a) Transport cost (b) Trade barriers
    (c) Exchange control (d) All the above.

29. According to Murika, the size of the capital depends on the

(a) Level of income (b) Level of savings
(c) Level or productivity (d) None of the above.

30. Capital to buy means capacity to produce is analogous to

(a) Say law (b) Law of supply
(c) Law of demand (d) Law of Keynes.

31. The techniques of production in underdeveloped countries are:

(a) Modern (b) Backward
(c) Semimodern (d) Ultra modren.

32. The basic feature of an underveloped country is

(a) Low per capital income
(b) Low productivity
(c) High level productivity
(d) All the above.

33. Industrialization in the LDC's is

(a) Inclave type
(b) Capital intensive
(c) Accommodative type
(d) Laour intensive.

34. Who wrote the book Poverty and Unbritish rule in India

(a) Romesh Chandra Dutt
(b) P.C. Joshi
(c) Surendar Nath Banerjee
(d) Dadabahi naroji.

35. Industry recorded a rent growth rates of

(a) 5% per annum (b) 5.4% per annum
(c) 6% per annum (d) 6.4% per annum.

36. In the Agricultural society, the output has increased at the rate of ...... % per annum over the plan period

(a) 2% (b) 2.2%
(c) 3% (d) 3.5%.

37. The tertiary sector accounts for about-or the labour force
    (a) 1/3rd (b) 1/4th
    (c) 1/5th (d) 1/6th.

38. The ratio of labour to both land and capital in agriculture showed a tendency to
    (a) Rise
    (b) Fall
    (c) Remain constant
    (d) None of these above.

39. The marginal productivity of labour in agriculture in India has turned out to be
    (a) Positive (b) Negative
    (c) Zero (d) Infinity.

40. To raise output per man hour requires raising to the ratio of
    (a) Capital to labour
    (b) Capital to output
    (c) Labour to capital
    (d) Labour to total fallen availability.

41. 'Socialist pattern of society' was envisaged in the
    (a) First plan (b) Second plan
    (c) Third plan (d) Fourth plan.

42. Over the period spanning from 1951 to 1981, industrial sector's share of absorbing labour force has increased by
    (a) 5% (b) 4%
    (c) 3% (d) 5%.

43. Which of the following industry developed well before independence
    (a) Heavy engineering (b) Machine tools
    (c) Chemical industries (d) Textile.

44. The per capita income of India, estimated in dollar terms in 1989 was merely
    (a) $320 (b) $330
    (c) $340 (d) $350.

45. The rate of capital accummulation before independence was just
    (a) 5% of national income
    (b) 6% of national income
    (c) 7% of national income
    (d) 8% of national income.

46. In percentage terms, the share of agriculture and primary activities in India's GDP over the planning
    (a) 56.4% (b) 45.5%
    (c) 39.5% (d) 33.9%.

47. Of the total production in the manufacturing sector in 1980-85, small scale sector accounted for about
    (a) 30% (b) 40%
    (c) 50% (d) 60%.

48. Per annum trend growth rules of service sector is around
    (a) 5% (b) 6%
    (c) 7% (d) 8%.

49. The share of public administration and defence in the GDP is
    (a) Steadily rising (b) Falling proportionately
    (c) Remaining unchanged (d) Unaccountable.

50. The growth shares of the services sector in the GDP reflect the expansion of
    (a) Agriculture in the country
    (b) Foreign trade
    (c) Economic infrastructure
    (d) Public sector in the economy.

51. The disguised unemployment in rural sector has tended to become widespread in recent years because the technical progress has become more and more
    (a) Capital intensive
    (b) Labour intensive
    (c) Import intensive
    (d) Both (a) & (b).

52. In broad, the term colonialism relates to

(a) Exploitation

(b) Exploitation of the upper caste to lower one

(c) Foreign domination

(d) Urban rural gap in the process of development.

ANSWERS

1.	(b)	2.	(c)	3.	(b)	4.	(b)
5.	(b)	6.	(d)	7.	(a)	8.	(d)
9.	(a)	10.	(d)	11.	(b)	12.	(a)
13.	(b)	14.	(c)	15.	(c)	16.	(d)
17.	(c)	18.	(c)	19.	(a)	20.	(c)
21.	(c)	22.	(a)	23.	(b)	24.	(d)
25.	(c)	26.	(d)	27.	(c)	28.	(d)
29.	(c)	30.	(a)	31.	(b)	32.	(d).
33.	(a)	34.	(a)	35.	(b)	36.	(b)
37.	(a)	38.	(a)	39.	(b)	40.	(a)
41.	(b)	42.	(c)	43.	(d)	44.	(d)
45.	(a)	46.	(a)	47.	(d)	48.	(a)
49.	(a)	50.	(c)	51	(d)	52.	(a)

SET 13
ASSESS YOURSELF

1. India's fiscal policy since Independence has centred around
   (a) More borrowings (b) Higher taxation
   (c) Deficit financing (d) All the three.
2. Fiscal Policy in a developing country like India aims at
   (a) Widening the tax base
   (b) Mopping up most of the surpluses through taxation
   (c) Achieving socio-economic objective of state
   (d) All of these.
3. The Ninth Finance Commission was appointed in
   (a) April 1985 (b) June 1987
   (c) April 1988 (d) March 1989.
4. The revenue of the state governments are raised from the following sources except one, which is that
   (a) Land revenue
   (b) Agricultural income tax
   (c) Entertainment tax
   (d) Expenditure tax.
5. The Ninth Finance Commission was headed by
   (a) Y.B. Chavan (b) Raja Chelliah
   (c) A.S. Qureshi (d) N.K.P. Salve.
6. Union government ensures expenditure on
   (a) Administrative services only

(b) Economic services only
(c) Both the above
(d) All of the above.

7. The most important source of plan finance to cover up the gap between intended expenditure and available resources is
(a) Deficit financing (b) Direct taxes
(c) Indirect taxes (d) Foreign aid.

8. Aid to India from the east European countries has largely taken the form of
(a) Investment in the public sector
(b) Loans to private sector
(c) Grants to the public enterprises
(d) Aid through trade.

9. Loans to foreign governments is
(a) Revenue expenditure
(b) Capital expenditure
(c) Both revenue and capital expenditure
(d) Neither revenue nor capital expenditure.

10. Central assistance for state and UT plans is a part of
(a) Plan expenditure
(b) Non plan expenditure
(c) Revenue expenditure
(d) None of the above.

11. If external debt of country rises faster than as interest obligations, it is a case of
(a) Liquidity trap (b) Debt trap
(c) Poverty trap (d) Export led growth.

12. The ninth Finance Commission recommended that share of the union territories in the net distributable procees of income tax should be —
(a) 1.437 (b) 1.903
(c) 1.734 (d) 1.309.

13. Debt relief to the farmers is part of
    (a) Plan expenditure
    (b) Non-plan expenditure
    (c) Development expenditure
    (d) All of the above.

14. Largest amount of resources for financing the five year plans in India is raised through
    (a) Taxation
    (b) Surplus of public enterprise
    (c) Deficit financing
    (d) External assistance.

15. The major sources of the government saving are given below one of them is wrong, which?
    (a) Taxes
    (b) Surplus of public enterprises
    (c) Transfer payments
    (d) Mobilisation of internal loan and deposits.

16. The basis of corporate tax is
    (a) Total turnover of the company
    (b) Profit after distribution of dividend
    (c) Profit before distribution of dividend
    (d) Capital employed in the company.

17. India has currently a
    (a) Deficit with EEC but surplus with Japan
    (b) Surplus with EEC but deficit with Japan
    (c) Surplus with the U.S.A and Russia
    (d) Deficit with the U.S.A. and a surplus with EEC.

18. Expenditure on general services is
    (a) Revenue expenditure
    (b) Capital expenditure
    (c) Plan expenditure
    (d) None of the above.

19. Which of the following is the biggest source of financing the seventh plan?
    (a) Additional taxes
    (b) Borrowing from the bank building the RBI.
    (c) Surplus of public enterprises
    (d) Foreign trade.

20. Which of the following taxes is levied by the Centre but wholly assigned to the states
    (a) Personal income tax
    (b) Excise on drugs and narcotics
    (c) Railway passenger tax
    (d) Gift tax.

21. According to the commendations of the Ninth Finance Commission—per cent of the divisible pool of income tax should be assigned to the states
    (a) 80 (b) 85
    (c) 90 (d) 92.

22. Food and fertilizer subsidies are included in
    (a) Capital expenditure
    (b) Revenue expenditure
    (c) Plan expenditure
    (d) All of the above.

23. Gross tax revenue of the union government is about of the national income at current prices
    (a) 25 per cent (b) 22 per cent
    (c) 18 per cent (d) 16 per cent.

24. Which of the following taxes have the largest share in the gross tax revenue of the union government?
    (a) Custom duties (b) Excise duties
    (c) Income tax (d) Wealth tax.

25. In a ______ budget revenue equals expenaiture
    (a) Surplus (b) Deficit
    (c) Balanced (d) None of the above.

26. Union excise duties contribute the largest amount to the central revenues their share in gross tax revenue of the union government is about

(a) 63 per cent (b) 43 per cent
(c) 33 per cent (d) 25 per cent.

27. Which of the following taxes is levied by the state government only

(a) Entertainment tax (b) Wealth tax
(c) Income tax (d) Corporation tax.

28. Which of the following taxes is levied by the state and shared with the union government

(a) Irrigation tax (b) Agriculture income
(c) Entertainment tax (d) None of the above.

29. Union Excise Duties are a part of central government

(a) Tax revenue (b) Non tax revenue
(c) Capital receipts (d) None of the above.

30. Revenue expenditure forms about .... of the total expenditure of the union government

(a) 60 per cent (b) 70 pe rcent
(c) 75 per cent (d) 80 per cent.

31. Of the gross tax revenue of the union government indirect taxes account for about

(a) 70 per cent (b) 75 per cent
(c) 80 per cent (d) 85 per cent.

32. Biggest source of capital receipts of the union government is

(a) Market borrowings (b) External assistance
(c) Small saving (d) Provident fund.

33. Which of the following is not a direct tax?

(a) Tax income
(b) Tax on wealth
(c) Tax on expenditure
(d) Tax on entertainment.

34. Excise duties, which are the biggest source of revenue of the union government, are levied on

(a) Sale of goods (b) Production of goods
(c) Consumption of goods (d) Resale of goods.

35. Who appoints the Finance Commission?

(a) President of India
(b) Prime Minister of India
(c) Chairman of Rajya Sabha
(d) Speaker of Lok Sabha.

36. The controlling authority of government expenditure is

(a) Reserve Bank of India
(b) Planning Commission
(c) Finance Minister
(d) Finance Commission.

37. Defence expenditure is about . . . . . . percent of the national income at current price

(a) 5 per cent (b) 6 per cent
(c) 8 per cent (d) 10 per cent.

38. Which one of the following taxes is not levied by the state governments

(a) Agricultural income tax
(b) Profession tax
(c) Excise on liquor
(d) Corporation tax.

39. MODVAT means

(a) Modified value added tax
(b) Moderate value added tax
(c) Modest value added tax
(d) Modern value added tax.

40. "Indian Tax Reform" is a book written by

(a) A.M. Khusro (b) T.K. Mehta
(c) P.R. Brahma Nanda (d) N. Kaldor.

41. In India, the states get maximum income from
    (a) Sales tax
    (b) Land Revenue
    (c) Agricultural income tax
    (d) State excise tax.

42. The union government collects largest share of revenue from
    (a) Direct taxes (b) Indirect taxes
    (c) Foreign aid (d) Deficit financing.

43. Interest payment is an item of
    (a) Revenue expenditure (b) Capital expenditure
    (c) Plan expenditure (d) None of the above.

44. The single largest donor to India has been
    (a) The World Bank (b) Japan
    (c) U.S.A. (c) Kuwait.

45. Largest source of non-tax revenue of the Union Government is
    (a) Surplus from public enterprises
    (b) Contribution of railways
    (c) Profit of RBI
    (d) Interest receipts

46. Of the total public debt internal debt accounts for about . . . . . . per cent
    (a) 60 (b) 70
    (c) 80 (d) 90.

47. The Income Tax Act which is now in force was commenced in the year
    (a) 1982 (b) 1961
    (c) 1971 (d) None of those.

48. The index number of wholesale prices showed a distinct decline during
    (a) First Plan (b) Second Plan
    (c) Fourth Plan (d) Fifth Plan.

49. Inflation tends to hit most
    (a) The speculators
    (b) The fixed wage earner
    (c) The share holders of companies
    (d) All of the above.

50. The sharpest rise in price in the post-Independence period was recorded during
    (a) 1960-65 (b) 1965-70
    (c) 1972-75 (d) 1985-90.

ANSWERS

1.	(d)	2.	(d)	3.	(b)	4.	(d)
5.	(d)	6.	(d)	7.	(a)	8.	(d)
9.	(b)	10.	(a)	11.	(b)	12.	(a)
13.	(b)	14.	(a)	15.	(c)	16.	(c)
17.	(a)	18.	(a)	19.	(c)	20.	(b)
21.	(b)	22.	(d)	23.	(c)	24.	(c)
25.	(b)	26.	(a)	27.	(d)	28.	(a)
29.	(c)	30.	(c)	31.	(a)	32.	(d)
33.	(b)	34.	(a)	35.	(c)	36.	(c)
37.	(a)	38.	(b)	39.	(a)	40.	(d)
41.	(a)	42.	(b)	43.	(a)	44.	(c)
45.	(d)	46.	(c)	47.	(b)	48.	(b)
49.	(d)	50.	(c)				